SCOTLAND ON A PLATE

First published 2001
by Black & White Publishing Ltd, Edinburgh
ISBN 1 902927 20 6
Introduction © Ferrier Richardson 2001
Text & Recipes © The Contributors 2001
Photographs © Alan Donaldson 2001

British Library Cataloguing in Catalogue Data:
A catalogue record for this book is available from the British Library.

Design concept by Navy Blue

Printed in Spain by Bookprint S.L.

SCOTLAND ON A PLATE

EDITED BY FERRIER RICHARDSON

Photographs by Alan Donaldson

IN ASSOCIATION WITH THE

sundayherald

Contents

3   **Laurie Black**
Fouters Bistro

13   **Geoffrey Botterill & Antony Butterworth**
Kilmichael Country House Hotel

23   **Nicola & Keith Braidwood**
Braidwoods

33   **Trevor Brooks**
Kinnaird

43   **Stewart Cameron**
Turnberry Hotel

53   **Alan Craigie**
The Creel

63   **Lesley Crosfield & Colin Craig**
The Albannach

75   **Andrew Fairlie**
Andrew Fairlie at Gleneagles

85   **Ian Ferguson & Stephen Steele**
Brig O'Doon

95   **Peter Fleming**
Cameron House

105 **Neil Forbes**
Atrium

115 **Jimmy & Amanda Graham**
Ostlers Close

125 **Simon Haigh & Matthew Gray**
Inverlochy Castle

135 **Andrew Hamer**
Gleneagles

147 **Tony Heath**
Let's Eat

157 **Peter Jukes**
The Cellar

167 **Patricia & Tim Martin**
Scarista House

177 **Wendy and Don Matheson & Charlie Lockley**
Boath House

187 **Donald McInnes, Andrew Costley,
Laurent Labede & Bruce Boyd**
Lochgreen House

199 **Ian McNaught & Eric Brown**
The Roman Camp

209 **Nick Nairn**
Nairns and Nairns Cook School

219 **Ferrier Richardson & Steven Caputa**
Eurasia

229 **Shirley Spear**
The Three Chimneys

241 **Mike Stoddart & Eddie McDonald**
The Marcliffe at Pitfodels

251 **David Wilson**
The Peat Inn

262 **Location Map**

263 **Contributor Details**

264 **Index**

We have reproduced recipes as supplied by the chefs,
according to their own individual cooking style.
All recipes serve four, unless otherwise stated.

Introduction

Three years on from surveying the restaurant scene of my own wonderful city in the first *Glasgow on a Plate*, we have arrived at the fourth book in the series, *Scotland on a Plate*.

Scotland as a nation has never been short of wonderful ingredients, be it beef, lamb, game, shellfish or seafood. Add to that some wonderful dairy produce, tasty root vegetables and, of course, the odd nip of whisky, and you can safely say that we have one of the finest natural larders of any country in the world.

Throughout Scotland we now have an array of talented chefs, from the classically trained to the gifted and experienced amateur. Years of hard work and dedication have brought them to the top of their chosen profession, and they are a credit to it and to Scotland.

Over the last twenty years, there have been many role models for young chefs rising through the ranks, none more so than David Wilson of the Peat Inn in Fife. Here is a man who is passionate about good food and wine, and knows all there is to know about the best local, natural produce, and when and how to cook it. In addition, his commitment to passing on this knowledge and enthusiasm has made a significant contribution to the healthy state of Scottish cooking today.

Scotland on a Plate not only provides a great selection of recipes, but also insight into the philosophy of each chef. We discover how they learned to cook, and how they manage day by day, making the most of their staff, and of the produce available, cooking for regular local diners and for visitors from all over the world.

I hope you enjoy reading this book and cooking the recipes, but I would also encourage you to visit the restaurants featured in *Scotland on a Plate*. This way, you will experience for yourself the finest of dining experiences, and also enjoy the magnificent scenery that makes Scotland such a wonderful place to live and to visit.

Finally, I would like to thank Alan Donaldson for some fantastic photography, once again, Siobhan Edwards for pulling the project together, and all the team at Black & White Publishing for their support.

Ferrier.

Laurie Black
Fouters Bistro

I started my career as a CID officer with the Metropolitan Police. I got interested in restaurants because I spent so much time talking to chef/proprietors about the cheque fraud that was going on – it was in the days before the cheque guarantee card, and cheque fraud was a big problem in London. The great thing was that the restaurateurs were only free to see me at the end of business and, when they did, they tended to cook me something tasty! At the same time, I made friends with Bob White who came from Troon. We decided to leave London and to set up a restaurant in Ayr. After five years in the Police, I just felt there was a different and better way of living. We opened Fouters Bistro on 16th December 1973 and have been going strong ever since. My wife and partner, Fran has managed front of house from the start. She came to work here part-time when Fouters opened; that's how we met. We've got wonderful dedicated customers, locally and from all over the world; people often talk about coming to "Laurie and Fran's" for dinner, rather than Fouters!

Our first chef, Hans Muller, came from Switzerland. I worked with him in the kitchen and learned a lot. I had always loved cooking and pouring over cookery books – Robert Carrier was a big influence. I've learned from every chef we've had here. At Fouters, our approach has been to use the best raw ingredients and the best of every season's produce. Food is a gift, to be understood and revered. Simplicity and taste are key.

I'm very involved in tourism in Scotland. I've been Chairman of 'Taste of Scotland' for seven years, and I'm also Vice-Chairman of the local tourism forum – a kind of self-help group for Ayrshire caterers, businesses, colleges. I'm very keen to encourage young people to think about careers in this industry; we have to persuade their parents and Careers Advisors too. The government is putting a lot of emphasis on tourism in Scotland, but it's not funding training. There's no future for tourism in Scotland unless we can attract good people into hospitality at all levels.

Laurie Black
Fouters Bistro

Parfait of chicken livers
with brandy and cream

450g fresh chicken livers
150g butter
1 small onion, chopped
2 cloves of garlic, crushed
1 pinch of dried thyme
salt and black pepper
115ml double cream
25ml each of brandy, red wine and
sherry
(Serves 6)

This fine pâté has been enjoyed at Fouters for the last twenty-seven years. When made with care it will please at any time – dressed up for that special occasion or enjoyed simply as a snack or canapé.

The recipe is for a generous starter for six; it will multiply up well and will keep for 5–6 days in the fridge and freezes well for up to one month. Check chicken livers carefully for any sign of green bile sac. This should have been removed, but occasionally it will be left. It is vital that this is not present and that it has not discoloured any of the liver – the sac contains bile, which will wreck the pâté. Place the livers in a dish and cover with cold milk to remove any impurities. Drain before cooking.

Meanwhile put butter, onions and garlic into a good-sized stainless-steel pan, put on to heat and gently sweat onion and garlic until they are soft but not coloured. Now add thyme and drained livers.

Cook on a medium heat for approximately 10 minutes, stirring regularly. The livers should be coloured on the outside, but still a little pink inside. When cooked, remove from the heat, add salt and pepper to taste – remembering to slightly over-season because once cooled the seasoning can be a little subdued – stir in the brandy, wine and sherry, and add the cream.

Now liquidise until very smooth; in a blender is best. It is important that the pâté is totally free of lumps. You could pass it through a sieve at this point just to make sure there are no lumps. Now pour the pâté into the chosen moulds, allow to cool, then cover and refrigerate until needed.

When it is time to serve, the pâté may be cut as in a slice, scooped with hot soup spoons or served in individual ramekin dishes. Serve dressed up with a selection of colourful leaves, some fruit, a drizzle of olive oil and reduced balsamic vinegar and toasted brioche, or wholemeal bread. Most white wines will go well with this starter, especially a good Chardonnay.

West Coast scallops

with saffron mash in a chive butter sauce

50g carrots, cut into batons
450g potatoes, mashed
pinch of saffron
20 scallops
2 tbsp vegetable oil
100g butter
splash of white wine
juice of 1 lemon
juice of ½ lime
salt and pepper
small bunch of chives, chopped
10g leek julienne, deep-fried

Scallops feature on our menus at Fouters as we are fortunate to have a plentiful supply on the west coast. It is very important to buy fresh scallops that have not been 'dipped' or soaked. This practice causes the scallops to swell up and increase in weight due to the liquid. Then, when cooked, the liquid comes out, spoiling the cooking process and resulting in much smaller, flabby scallops. Scallops, like most seafood, require the minimum of cooking, as you will see.

Earlier in the day, cook carrots and any other vegetables you fancy (French beans work well), and make mashed potatoes. Just before cooking scallops, add saffron to creamed potatoes. Heat a little butter in a non-stick pan to reheat vegetables quickly when needed.

Pat the scallops dry. Heat a heavy-bottomed sauté or frying pan. Add vegetable oil (it will fry at a higher temperature than olive oil and so brown the scallops well). When the oil is almost smoking, carefully add scallops, not too many at a time; they must not touch or the steam from the cooking process will cause the oil to dilute and so stew rather than fry the scallops (or any other fish or meat you may be cooking). Cook on each side for about 1 or 2 minutes, depending on size.

Meanwhile, heat the butter in a pan with white wine, lemon and lime juice and seasoning. At the last minute add chopped chives – it is important that the herb goes in for just a few seconds so as to retain its colour and flavour.

To serve, arrange creamed potatoes in centre of plate, with scallops and carrot batons on top. Then spoon a little of the sauce between the scallops, not over, so as to preserve their crispness. Top creamed potato with deep-fried leek.

Laurie Black
Fouters Bistro

Carrick lamb
with fine ratatouille and orange honey sauce

for the ratatouille
2 tbsp olive oil
1 small onion
2 cloves garlic
1 courgette
1 small aubergine
2 tbsp tomato puree
freshly ground black pepper
rock salt
½ tsp sugar

for the lamb
1 tbsp olive oil
salt and pepper
4 x 150g loin fillet of lamb or 8
lamb cutlets
275ml lamb or general meat stock
splash of white wine
1 tbsp honey
100ml fresh orange juice
zest of 1 orange
25g cold butter
5cm square pieces of red, green,
yellow or orange peppers, cut into
small dice, to garnish

Ask your butcher for lamb that has been hung for at least one week – so often meat is sold too fresh and only disappoints, so it is with a serious note that I ask you to speak to your butcher and to develop a relationship with him. Tell him what you want. If he provides it, tell him. If he does not, tell him you will only give him your custom if he makes the effort to sell quality well-hung meat to you. After all, just look at the price – you deserve the best! Now I have that off my chest, to continue
. . . Ideally you want loin of lamb taken off the bone and cut into 150g pieces. Should this be a problem, use lamb cutlets.

The ratatouille can be prepared earlier and warmed through when serving the lamb.
For the ratatouille: finely dice vegetables. Heat olive oil in a heavy pan and gently fry onion and garlic. Do not allow to colour. When softish, add all the other ingredients, freshly ground pepper, rock salt and a little sugar. Cook on a slow simmer until vegetables are almost cooked. Remove and allow to cool.
For the lamb: Heat a little oil in a heavy sauté or frying pan. Season lamb and pan-fry for 2–3 minutes on both sides. Remove from heat and place in a warm oven. Add stock and wine to pan and bubble up. Add honey, orange juice and zest. Check seasoning. When good coating consistency, remove from heat and gradually beat cold butter into sauce to help thicken and give a little shine to the sauce.
To serve, spoon ratatouille in small pile on hot plates. Carve each piece of lamb and arrange on top of ratatouille. Serve with gratin dauphinoise potatoes cut out of baking tray, and arrange a little of diced pepper around base of potatoes. Finish by carefully pouring a little sauce over lamb and drizzle on plate.
Serve any extra sauce in a sauceboat. For hearty appetites, extra vegetables can be served either on the side or under the lamb.

Fouters iced soufflé

with Grand Marnier

275ml double cream
200g castor sugar
2 large egg yolks
50ml liqueur
for the garnish
dusting of chocolate powder
or cocoa mixed 50/50 with
castor sugar
some whipped double cream
seasonal fruits
dusting of icing sugar

(Serves 6)

This simple-to-make pudding can be dressed up for a dinner party or served simply for a family treat. This recipe uses Grand Marnier liqueur, but you could use any of your favourite liqueurs.

The prepared mixture can be either poured into one large ramekin or individual ramekins for serving.

Whip double cream to soft peaks. Add castor sugar and beat a little more.

In a separate bowl, beat egg yolks with liqueur, then add immediately to cream. Stir in well. Then pour in ramekin dishes.

Put in freezer and freeze for at least 12 hours. Remove from freezer and place in fridge half an hour before serving.

For a real treat, scoop out a small amount from top of ramekin and place to side, then fill hole with neat liqueur!

Geoffrey Botterill and Antony Butterworth
Kilmichael Country House Hotel

Antony and I met while teaching in the Middle East twenty years ago and we have worked all over the world both before and since then. We came to Arran ten years ago, not really to open a hotel, but to do up an historic house with a garden and outbuildings. Architecture has always been an interest of mine, and both of us wanted a new challenge. Initially, we saw Kilmichael as a base from which to travel abroad, but the hotel seems to have developed a momentum of its own and taken over our lives by stealth! Even so, the priority has always been to retain the look and feel of a private house, a characteristic which guests seem to particularly appreciate.

As cooks, we are self-taught and enthusiastic though not, I hope, obsessive. When we opened, I did all the cooking but, after about a year, Antony took over – he likes hiding in the kitchen! We have learned a lot as we have gone along. Having travelled, we know a fair bit about food, so we bring in our experience of flavours and combinations – and we do like to offer the adventurous and unexpected, from time to time. Having said that, Antony is particularly fond of traditional foods such as kidneys, and damsons. Puddings are an important part of the meal at Kilmichael since they are the final taste that people take away with them.

Whenever possible, we use the best quality local ingredients – of which there is a very wide range on the island – but, as you would expect, we also bring in things from elsewhere to maintain the highest standards. We tend to be perfectionist – being very self-critical – but are not remotely interested in food fashion and fads – particularly the prevailing British fashion for analysing or 'inspecting' a meal, rather than enjoying it in the Continental way. Food is, of course, very important, but you need to keep a sense of proportion. As one very down-to-earth friend said, "At the end of the day, you're just giving them their tea!" We want our guests to really enjoy "their tea", but in a peaceful, relaxed and friendly atmosphere.

Hot spiced Arran crab

4 medium-sized crabs
3 small cloves of garlic, peeled and finely chopped
240g butter
2 small anchovy fillets, chopped
$1/4$ tsp cayenne pepper
juice of $1/2$ lemon
3 tbsp white wine
$1/2$ tsp fresh coriander, finely chopped
$1/4$ tsp freshly grated nutmeg
1 tbsp fresh thyme or oregano, chopped
90g fresh white breadcrumbs
1 tbsp fresh parsley, chopped
2 leeks, sliced lengthways into 6 inch strips

Use only fresh boiled crab for this dish: ready-prepared crab meat tends to taste stale in comparison, even after the addition of spices. We use Sophie Grigson's humane method and chill live crabs for 2 hours in the freezer so that they are comatose when plunged into boiling water.

Boil crabs for 20 minutes after plunging them into fast boiling water containing 100g salt per litre. Extract all meat, initially keeping white and brown meat separate. Wash shells and save legs for garnishing.

Gently soften garlic in 15g of butter for 1–2 minutes. Add anchovies and cayenne and cook for a minute more. Add lemon juice and wine.

Remove from heat and stir in coriander, nutmeg and thyme, and two-thirds of breadcrumbs. Add brown crab meat and half of remaining butter.

Return to heat and, when heated through, add white crab meat. Add enough of remaining butter and breadcrumbs to achieve a moist (but not too soft), rich and buttery mixture. Finally, stir in half of the chopped parsley just before serving.

Steam leeks until tender and add a little butter.

Fill bottom of crab shells with leeks, and spoon a quarter of crab mixture into each. Sprinkle parsley on top and serve, with reserved legs to garnish.

Geoffrey Botterill and Antony Butterworth
Kilmichael Country House Hotel

Kidneys with two mustards

for the blinis

170g plain flour
60g wholemeal flour
7g (1 packet) easybake instant yeast
1 tsp salt
1 tsp sugar
285ml warm milk
1 egg, separated

for the kidneys

1 tbsp melted butter or cream
100g mushrooms, sliced –
including chanterelles, if available
50g butter
8 lamb's kidneys, split and cleaned
½ tbsp Arran wholegrain mustard
½ tbsp Dijon mustard
2 tbsp double cream
1 orange, segmented
2 tbsp soured cream
watercress, to serve
rocket, to serve

For the blinis: put all dry ingredients into food processor and, with motor running, add milk and egg yolk. Mix until smooth, pour into a bowl and leave covered for 45 minutes in a warm place. Fold in butter/cream. Whisk egg white until stiff and fold in too. Leave to prove for a further 10 minutes.

Cook a ladleful at a time in a hot, dry pan, turning when the top starts to bubble. Keep warm.

Lightly sauté mushrooms in butter. Remove from pan and keep warm. Sauté kidneys quickly until lightly browned. Add mustards and cream, together with mushrooms and orange segments. Allow to bubble gently until orange is warmed through.

Serve on warm blini with soured cream and a few leaves of watercress and rocket.

Chicken tournedos
stuffed with oak-smoked West Coast mussels

for the stuffing
1 litre fresh West Coast mussels
2 rashers Ayrshire bacon
1 Cox apple, peeled, cored and diced
15g butter
4–6 fresh sage leaves, roughly chopped
salt and pepper

for the sauce
1 shallot, finely chopped
1 clove of garlic, finely chopped
15g butter
400ml dry vermouth
liquid from smoked mussels made up to 300ml with chicken stock
150ml double cream

for the tournedos
5 x 200g chicken breasts, boned and skinned
2 tbsp double cream
15g butter, plus extra for greasing
sage leaves for garnish

The idea for making 'tournedos' from chicken, or indeed lamb or pork, comes from Gary Rhodes. This dish can be made with commercially bought smoked mussels, although the flavour will not be so fresh or subtle.

For the stuffing: smoke mussels over oak chips, reserving the liquid (you could make a smoker by placing mussels on a rack in a roasting tin inside a larger roasting tin containing water, on top of heat). Allow to cool and shell all except 12 of the best for garnish. Chop coarsely. Grill and finely chop bacon. Lightly sauté apple in butter, add chopped sage, bacon and mussel meat. Season and leave to cool.

For the sauce: soften shallot and garlic in melted butter. Add vermouth and bring to boil, reducing by three-quarters. Add stock and reduce by two-thirds. Add cream and simmer for 5–10 minutes until thickened. Season to taste.

For the tournedos: remove sinew from chicken breasts and discard. Blend one breast with a little cream in the food processor to make a paste. Slice remaining breasts horizontally into 2 or 3 flat pieces. Lay out 40cm square piece of foil, buttered. Cover it with piece of buttered baking parchment cut to same size. Spread pieces of chicken slices, slightly overlapping, to measure 20 x 22cm. Cover with chicken paste and then spread mussel mixture evenly on top. Roll up chicken using foil and parchment round outside of chicken and twisting ends to form a sausage shape. Chill for 2–3 hours.

Preheat oven to 200°C/gas mark 6. Cut chicken parcel into 4 pieces with sharp knife and tie string around each one to prevent it falling apart while cooking. Discard end pieces of parcel. Melt butter in pan and brown both sides of chicken tournedos. Roast for 15 minutes. Remove and rest for 5 minutes. Discard foil, parchment and string.

Deep-fry sage leaves in hot oil; as soon as crisped up sprinkle with salt. Serve chicken on a bed of courgette ribbons, poached leeks or buttered spinach. Garnish with deep-fried sage leaves and reserved mussels.

Geoffrey Botterill and Antony Butterworth
Kilmichael Country House Hotel

A gin and damson sundae

for the damson fool

700g damsons

150ml water

400g granulated sugar

4 tbsp gin

285ml double cream (or half cream
and home-made proper custard)

8 ratafia biscuits or 2 boudoir
biscuits broken into 8 pieces

**for the damson and soured
cream ice cream**

250ml double cream

250ml soured cream

half damson puree

**for Mrs Crook's orange and
hazelnut shortbread**

500g butter

500g plain flour

250g cornflour

250g icing sugar

50g hazelnuts, chopped

grated rind of 1 orange

for garnish

4 tbsp whipped cream

4 sprigs of fresh mint

8 damsons, sliced

for the damson gin

500g damsons, rinsed and pricked
with a needle

500g sugar

700ml gin

This recipe works equally well with other sharp fruit such as gooseberries or rhubarb.

For the damson fool: rinse damsons and bring to the boil with water. Add sugar and cook gently, covered, for 5–10 minutes or until damsons are soft. Allow to cool and rub through a plastic sieve. Add gin and chill resulting purée.

Whip cream (or cream and custard) until stiff and fold in half damson purée, reserving 4 dessertspoons. Put a couple of ratafia biscuits into the bottom of 4 tall glasses. Add a dessertspoon of reserved purée, and top with fool mixture. Chill.

For the damson and soured cream ice cream: whip two creams together until stiff. Fold in damson purée and either still freeze or churn in an ice-cream maker.

For Mrs Crook's orange and hazelnut shortbread: in food processor, mix all ingredients except hazelnuts. Once mixed, fold in hazelnuts. Cut mixture into small shapes (stars, hearts etc.). Bake at 180°C/gas mark 4, for 18–20 minutes. Sprinkle with castor sugar.

To serve, top prepared fools with small scoops of ice cream, whipped cream, mint leaves and slices of damson, accompanied by shortbread shapes, and damson gin – if you have had the foresight to make it. This is done by tightly sealing damsons, sugar and gin in a jar, keeping it in a dark place and shaking every couple of days for at least 3 weeks.

Nicola and Keith Braidwood
Braidwoods

Nicola: I grew up in a seaside resort, so there was always plenty of work in cafés and restaurant kitchens. I went to catering college at sixteen and, at eighteen, started working as a chef. Not long after Keith and I met, we realised our goal was to run our own place one day, but we knew it would take a long time.

Keith: I wanted to be a journalist, but then I didn't do very well in my English exams. We lived in Fife and my parents were regulars at the Peat Inn, and I ended up with a job working for David Wilson. That was a brilliant start; the Peat Inn has a great reputation and working for David certainly helps open doors. I was there for more than two years and then moved north to Inverlochy Castle. Before we opened Braidwoods in 1994, Nicola and I had learned lots of useful lessons about running a kitchen together, first at Murrayshall Hotel, outside Perth, with a brigade of eight chefs, and then – just the two of us – at Shieldhill Hotel in Biggar.

Nicola: Opening our own place was nerve-wracking, at first. We knew about cooking, but not about all the other things you need to know – like how to take credit card payments! And it was my first time away from the kitchen, front of house. It's all got easier with time, in that now we have lots of regulars. At Braidwoods we cook the food we'd like to eat; sometimes we'd love to come here to eat! We like being in Ayrshire; we didn't really know it before we moved, but this is a lovely spot. Quite isolated, I suppose, and sometimes we really need to get away to Glasgow or London – we love eating out.

Keith: Every chef dreams of having their own place and maybe of winning some accolades. We certainly did, but it takes time. In January 2000, we won a Michelin Star and, in October, we collected out third AA rosette. It couldn't be better, really, to have put a wee place like Dalry on the culinary map!

Escalope of hot smoked salmon

on a warm new potato, olive and herb salad with crème fraîche and caviar

250g new potatoes, cooked, diced and cold
125g plum tomatoes, skinned and diced
75g black kalamata olives, stoned and chopped
25g fresh basil, roughly chopped at last minute
4 x 75g escalopes of hot smoked salmon (or use cold smoked, lightly grilled)
for the dressing
6 tbsp lemon juice
18 tbsp virgin olive oil
sea salt and pepper
for the garnish
4 tbsp crème fraîche
caviar, to garnish (optional)

Mix together potato, tomatoes, olives and basil in a bowl.
Whisk lemon juice and oil to make dressing, seasoning to taste.
Add a little dressing to potato mixture and warm gently in pan – do not mash it up!
Divide salad mix and spoon on to the centre of each of 4 plates.
Place salmon on top and, on top of that, spoon crème fraîche and caviar if desired. To finish, spoon on a little extra dressing around the plate.
NB You can serve the salmon gently warmed or cold.

An Arbroath smokie
and saffron stew with medley of seafood

6 Arbroath smokies
1 onion
1 head of celery
1 leek
$^{1}/_{2}$ bulb of fennel
50g butter
pinch of saffron strands
$^{1}/_{2}$ litre dry white wine
$1^{1}/_{4}$ litres chicken stock
250ml double cream
250ml crème fraîche
4 x 25g white fish, e.g. brill, cod, turbot, sole
4 x 25g salmon pieces
4 scallops (large)
4 langoustines (large)
50g mussels
50g chives, chopped

For the smokie stew base (which can be made in advance): warm smokies in oven at 180°C/gas mark 4 for 30-40 minutes (to make it easier for skin and bones to be removed). Then separate flesh from skin and bones and set aside.

Finely chop onion, celery, leek and fennel.

Add butter to a heavy-based, large pan, and sweat off the vegetables – do not colour.

Add saffron and wine, and reduce until syrupy consistency. Add chicken stock and bring to the boil.

Add smokies, bones and flesh but not skin. Add cream and crème fraîche, and bring back to the boil.

Leave to cool and pass through a fine sieve.

When ready to serve, warm large bowls and heat smokie base gently. Add in fish, in order of length of cooking: white fish (2 minutes cooking required), salmon (1 minute), large scallops and langoustines (1 minute), mussels (30 seconds). By the time the stew is almost up to boiling point, take off the heat and add lashings of chopped chives.

To make more of a hearty meal, boiled potatoes cooked in saffron could be added.

Crisp roast confit of duck leg

with stir-fried vegetables and an oriental sauce

4 duck legs (in their own fat)
275ml rendered pork or goose fat
(fat and a little water reduced on a
low heat)
1 onion
2 carrots
2 shallots
6 cloves of garlic
2 bay leaves
1 sprig of thyme
1 sprig of tarragon
piece of orange rind
1 tsp black peppercorns
1 tsp allspice berries
6 juniper berries
4 tsp sea salt
coriander, to garnish

for the oriental sauce
125ml jellied stock
2 shallots, finely chopped
25g root ginger, finely chopped
1 star anise
2 dried chillies
1 tbsp hoi sin sauce
1 tbsp honey

for the stir-fry
1 tbsp vegetable oil
50g beansprouts
50g Chinese leaves, finely
shredded
50g carrot, finely shredded
50g red pepper, finely shredded
50g spring onion, finely shredded
50g button mushrooms, finely chopped
soy sauce

The day before, place all confit ingredients in a heavy-based pan with tight-fitting lid. Cook for 2–3 hours at 150°C/gas mark 2. Do not let the fat boil.

Remove from oven and allow to cool naturally overnight.

For the oriental sauce: from the pan in which you've cooked the duck legs, remove jellied stock. (If there's not 125ml stock, make up with chicken stock.)

Sweat shallot, ginger, anise and chilli in a little duck fat – do not colour. Add hoi sin and honey.

Reduce until sauce starts to thicken. Keep tasting, as it will become salty if over-reduced.

To serve, crisp up duck legs in a hot oven (200°C/gas mark 6) for 15–20 minutes.

Warm sauce in a pan.

Heat wok and stir-fry vegetables in a dash of vegetable oil.

Season with a little soy sauce, and spoon vegetables into middle of plate. Place duck on top, spoon a little of sauce around and garnish with fresh coriander.

Honey wafer millefeuilles of raspberries and nectarines

for the honey wafers
200g butter
100g icing sugar
100g plain flour
pinch of ground ginger
3 tbsp runny honey
2 egg whites
100g raspberries

for the crème mousseline
1/2 litre milk
1 vanilla pod, split
7 egg yolks
3 tbsp castor sugar
1 1/2 tbsp plain flour
250ml double cream, whipped

for the raspberry coulis
200ml water
200g castor sugar
500g frozen raspberries

4 nectarines, poached
250g fresh raspberries
4 sprigs of mint

For the honey wafers: place all ingredients in food processor until blended, then refrigerate. Preheat oven to 190°C/gas mark 5. Line baking tray with silicone paper. Thinly spread mix into 5cm round template (3 wafers per person). Bake until golden (approximately 5 minutes), then place on cooling tray.
NB The wafers are fragile, so make extra.
For the crème mousseline: bring milk and vanilla pod to the boil.
Meanwhile, whisk yolks, sugar and flour until pale, then pour hot milk on to egg mix. Stir together.
Return to pan and gently cook, stirring all the time, until mixture thickens. Place pan in iced water to cool as quickly as possible.
Take 8 tablespoons of cooled mixture and gently fold in same amount of whipped cream. Place in fridge until later.
For the raspberry coulis: bring water and sugar to the boil and add raspberries. Liquidise and pass through a fine sieve.

To serve, halve nectarines, and then cut each half into 3. In centre of each plate, put a small spoonful of crème mousseline. Place first honey wafer layer.
On wafer, arrange nectarine slices and a few raspberries, then spoonful of mousseline and next wafer. Repeat.
Add the last wafer and garnish with a few more raspberries, a sprig of fresh garden mint and pour a few spoonfuls of coulis around the plate.

Trevor Brooks
Kinnaird

I wasn't really planning to be a chef. I was taking an HND course in Building Management when I saw a job as a trainee chef – no qualifications required – and started thinking that cooking might be a good thing to get into. I got a job at Portmeirion in North Wales, where the chef had been trained at Maxim's in Paris. I can't say I was any good at that stage, but I really enjoyed it and felt excited about the possibilities; I knew I wanted to go on and do as well as I could as a chef. The trouble was that I was already a bit too old – I tried to work for the Roux brothers, but I was twenty and their trainees were all sixteen. So, off I went to catering college, and afterwards, I was lucky enough to land a job at a Michelin starred restaurant in Germany. This was a great experience and really opened up avenues, and consequently jobs, in some of Britain's leading hotels, including Inverlochy Castle.

In 1987, my wife Jane and I opened our restaurant in Torquay. We ran that successfully for nine years: Jane front of house, and myself as cook and potwasher. By 1996, we needed a change of scene and so decided to move on and sell up.

The position at Kinnaird came pretty much out of the blue. I knew of the hotel by reputation and had followed its progress through guide books since its opening. I was delighted to be appointed Head Chef in 1998.

One of the most refreshing factors about my change of job is being able to work with other chefs again – it's very inspiring to share ideas. I try to keep the food we cook here simple, but interesting. It's all very much about the freshness of the ingredients, and about retaining the identity of those ingredients. We use Scottish produce as much as possible. The Kinnaird Estate – all 9,000 acres of it – provide an abundance of game. We are also developing our walled garden, which has been out of use for years; we grow our own herbs, salad leaves, vegetables and unusual potato varieties. We hope, in the future, to continue to improve the yield from our garden as much as possible, as it is great to have all these ingredients to hand pick according to our daily changing menus.

Trevor Brooks
Kinnaird

Asparagus mousse

with a garden herb salad and crab beignets

for the mousse

500g asparagus
2 shallots
1 clove of garlic
500ml vegetable stock
2 leaves of gelatine, soaked
150ml whipping cream

for the beignets

250g white crab meat
salt and pepper
$\frac{1}{2}$ tbsp lemon juice

for the batter

4 tbsp flour
2 tbsp cornflour
1 tbsp baking powder
ice-cold sparkling water

selection of soft garden herbs and
salad leaves, e.g. dill, tarragon,
chervil, flat-leaf parsley, coriander
olive oil

For the mousse: we use white asparagus, but green is fine.

Peel asparagus and remove woody base. Reserve. Place trimmings, shallots and garlic in stock and bring to the boil. Simmer to extract all flavour.

Sieve out trimmings, shallot and garlic and discard. Reduce liquid to 200ml.

Chop all remaining asparagus and add to liquid. Cook until tender; do not overcook or the colour will be lost. Liquidise and, while hot, add gelatine. Pass through a fine sieve. Allow to cool completely.

Whip cream to a soft peak stage and fold through cool purée.

Place into 4 moulds and chill until set.

For the beignets: season crab meat with salt, pepper and lemon juice. Shape into 12 small quenelles. Place in freezer to set completely.

For the batter: mix all ingredients together to form light batter.

To serve, unmould mousse into centre of plates. Dress salad leaves with olive oil and arrange on top of mousse.

Remove crab meat from freezer. Dip each quenelle into batter and deep-fry until golden (at 180°C for 4–5 minutes). Test centre of quenelle with tip of small knife to check internal temperature – ensure they are hot.

Arrange around mousse and serve.

Sea bass

with artichoke ravioli, tomato fondant and beurre blanc

4 globe artichoke hearts (all leaves, choke and stalk removed)
1 sprig of thyme
1 sprig of rosemary
2 shallots
1 tbsp olive oil
1 clove of garlic, finely chopped
200ml white wine
salt and pepper
2 plum tomatoes, coarsely diced
4 x fillets sea bass (each 180–200g)
1–2 tbsp olive oil
1 tbsp lemon juice

for the pasta dough
250g pasta flour
8–9 egg yolks
1 tbsp olive oil

for the tomato fondant
20 ripe plum tomatoes
2 shallots
2 cloves of garlic
1 tbsp olive oil
salt and pepper
4 basil leaves, shredded

for the chive oil
100g chives
salt and pepper
150ml olive oil

for the beurre blanc
1 shallot
1 clove of garlic
1 tbsp white wine vinegar
1 sprig of thyme
1 sprig of rosemary
2 tbsp white wine
250g butter, cubed and chilled
6 baby artichokes, for garnish (optional)
2 tbsp olive oil

Slice artichoke hearts thinly and finely chop shallots, thyme and rosemary.

Sauté artichoke in olive oil until lightly browned, add shallots, garlic, thyme and rosemary and cook until shallots soften. Add white wine, cover and steam until tender. Remove lid to allow remaining liquid to evaporate. Season and add chopped tomatoes. Allow to cool completely.

For the ravioli: mix ingredients together to form dough, kneading for several minutes. Refrigerate for 20 minutes.

Roll out dough into 150mm-wide band, 1–2mm thick.

Pile 4 domes of artichoke mix on half the dough, brush with water around domes (to ensure top layer of pasta sticks). Gently lay the other half of pasta strip over artichoke mix. Press pasta together around domes and cut out with a pastry cutter. Place on to silicone paper and refrigerate until needed.

For the tomato fondant: skin and deseed tomatoes and cut into rough dice. Finely chop shallots and garlic. Sweat shallots and garlic in olive oil until softened. Add tomato and cook over a low heat until all the moisture has evaporated and you are left with a thick tomato paste. Season and add basil. Keep warm.

For the chive oil: blanch chives in boiling, salted water and refresh immediately in iced water, then drain. Place into blender with a little salt and process, adding olive oil in a trickle. Check seasoning and pass through a fine sieve or muslin.

For the beurre blanc: chop shallot and garlic and add to a saucepan with vinegar, thyme and rosemary. Cook over high heat until evaporated. Add wine and boil until reduced by three-quarters. Remove from heat, then whisk in butter one piece at a time. Whisk until each piece has been emulsified. Pass through a fine sieve, cover with clingfilm and leave in a warm place.

To finish, pan-fry sea bass fillets in a little olive oil, skin side down, for 4–5 minutes over a moderate heat to crisp skin. Turn over, season with pepper, salt, and a squeeze of lemon. Allow to rest in pan to finish cooking on residual heat. Split baby artichokes in half, lengthways, remove choke and sauté in olive oil until tender.

Plunge ravioli into a large pot of boiling, salted water. Cook for 3–4 minutes, and remove. Drizzle with olive oil and keep warm.

Place tomato fondant in rings in centre of four large plates. Surround with beurre blanc. Top with a ravioli. Place sea bass on top, and put a ribbon of chive oil around beurre blanc. Serve immediately.

Trevor Brooks
Kinnaird

Fillet of Angus beef

with spinach, fondant potatoes, roasted cherry tomatoes
and deep-fried shallots

for the fondant potatoes
4 large potatoes, peeled and cut
into 12 equal cubes (approximately
2 x 2 x 2cm)
200g butter
salt and pepper

for the tempura batter
4 tbsp flour
2 tbsp cornflour
1 tbsp baking powder
ice-cold sparkling water
4 shallots, peeled and sliced into
rings
300ml vegetable oil

for the Madeira sauce
100g shallots
100g mushrooms, sliced
25g butter
1 tbsp sherry vinegar
200ml dry Madeira
100ml veal glace
1 sprig of thyme

4 x 175g fillet steaks, fully trimmed
1 tbsp olive oil
50g butter
500g spinach, washed and stalk
removed
12 cherry tomatoes on vine

For the fondant potatoes: colour tops of cubes in 50g butter in a frying pan. Place in an even layer into 3cm-deep saucepan, just large enough to hold all the potatoes. Add remaining butter and enough water to just below tops of potatoes. Season well, bring to the boil and cook rapidly until reduced by half. Place in moderate oven (170°C/gas mark 3) for 10-15 minutes, to complete absorption, and cooking. Remove and keep warm.

For the batter: Mix tempura ingredients to form a light batter. Do not over-mix. Pass shallots through batter, and deep-fry in vegetable oil in small saucepan. Set aside and keep warm.

For the Madeira sauce: sweat shallots and mushrooms together in butter, then increase heat to obtain a good caramel colouring. Add sherry vinegar and deglaze, scraping all deposits off bottom of pan and evaporate completely. Add Madeira and reduce by three-quarters. Add veal glace (reduced veal stock or reduced beef stock will do) and thyme. Reduce to a coating consistency. Season and pass through a fine sieve.

To finish, cook fillet steaks in olive oil and half the butter to your preference. Keep warm.

Melt remaining butter in a large saucepan, and fry spinach until well wilted. Season, drain and press between layers of kitchen paper to remove excess liquid, and keep warm.

Cut cherry tomatoes into 4 bunches of 3, still attached to vine. Drizzle with olive oil and place in hot oven (200°C/gas mark 6) for 2 minutes. Remove and sprinkle with sea salt. Keep warm.

Place a circle of spinach on one side of each plate. Place a fillet on top. On other side of plate, place 3 fondant squares. Balance tomatoes on top of potatoes. Put a pile of shallots on top of beef. Surround with sauce.

Trevor Brooks
Kinnaird

Vanilla soufflé

with summer berry sorbets

100g clarified butter
castor sugar, for dusting
for the soufflé base
5 vanilla pods split lengthways
400ml milk
2 egg yolks
40g sugar
40g cornflour
for the meringue mix
5 egg whites
90g sugar
for the tuille baskets
100g soft butter
225g flour
225g icing sugar
7 egg whites
pinch of salt

(Serves 6)

Prepare 6 individual soufflé pots by buttering twice with clarified butter, allowing the first layer to set in fridge first. Finally, coat inside with castor sugar and shake out excess.

Scrape out vanilla seeds into milk and bring to boil. In a bowl, whisk egg yolks and sugar together, then add cornflour. Whisk until light in colour, then gradually pour in strained hot milk, continuing to whisk until all incorporated. Pour into clean saucepan and return to simmer for approximately 2 minutes, while stirring. You should have a smooth, thick mixture. Cover with clingfilm and allow to cool at room temperature.

Then pour half into wide bowl (freeze rest for future use).

Whisk egg whites to soft peak stage and gradually add sugar, while still whisking to firm peaks. Add one-third meringue into base mix and amalgamate. Fold in remaining meringue with a metal spoon until well mixed. Spoon into prepared soufflé dishes and bake at 180°C/gas mark 5 for 8–10 minutes until well risen and golden on top. Dust with icing sugar.

For the tuille baskets: cream butter and add flour, sugar, egg whites and salt. Beat until a smooth batter is achieved. Spread out into individual thin circles with a teaspoon on a greased baking tray. Cook at approximately 180°C/gas mark 5 until golden brown (5–6 minutes).

Remove from oven and, when still hot, mould over dariole or similar mould. Allow to cool and carefully remove to an airtight container until required.

Our selection of summer berry sorbets includes blackcurrant, strawberry, tayberry and raspberry (any flavour would work well, home-made or bought).

Line a baking sheet with silicone paper and freeze. When chilled, remove from freezer and on it place small pearls of sorbet (with a small parisienne cutter or melon-baller). Put back in freezer until needed.

Place soufflé on to serving plates with tuille baskets containing sorbet pearls. Serve immediately.

Stewart Cameron
Turnberry Hotel

I've been Executive Chef at Turnberry for 20 years and I've worked in kitchens for over 40 years. My family were all farmers – I was brought up on a farm outside Dunblane – but my mother was against me going into the business. I'm not at all sure why I ended up in catering, but it must suit me!

I served my apprenticeship in British Transport Hotels (as they were in those days); my first kitchen was in the Lochalsh Hotel where the chef spoke no English and there were six nationalities in all. I hated it at first and was very homesick, but was allowed to go home for a weekend in the middle of the season and after that loved the job! I moved to the Caledonian Hotel in Edinburgh, working with a wonderful team of characters under an inspirational French chef, Edward Merard. Then on to the Ritz – in those days you had to have the London experience which, in the mid-1960s, was great fun, but I never had much money. For a break, I took a job in Bermuda, but I always knew I'd come back to Scotland. And after 18 months I did, coming back to work at Gleneagles, the Central Hotel in Glasgow and the Station Hotel in Perth, before moving to Turnberry. In the time I've been here, there's been a phenomenal amount of change – the last thing you could ever call this job is boring! When I retire, the one thing I'll really miss is the camaraderie. I've got a great team of chefs here: Colin Watson (Head Chef, is Swiss-trained and worked in the Bahamas for two years), Austen Reid (junior sous chef and member of the Scottish Culinary Olympic Team), and Colin Wilson (pastry chef, recently returned from Australia and Bermuda).

The current owners, Starwood, are investing in making Turnberry an all-round resort hotel, refurbishing all the rooms, developing a Golf Academy and redesigning one of the golf courses, as well as upgrading the spa facilities.

We have an international clientele, with a broad range of tastes and requirements. The main restaurant offers classical cooking, using modernised French-based methods; the brasserie serves lighter, Mediterranean-style food; while the clubhouse caters to golfer's wishes – a quick turnaround, and a range of food from full meals to sandwiches.

20g haricots blanc
20g each of green, brown, red
lentils
40g mirepoix (diced carrot, onion,
celery and leek)
20g garlic
80g smoked poitrine (bacon belly)
4 bay leaves
8 sprigs of thyme
40g butter
2 litres good chicken stock
200g Dover sole
75g sea bass (skin on, scaled)
75g red mullet (skin on, scaled)
75g salmon (skinned)
75g lobster
75g scampi
75g cockles
75g mussels
150g calamari
plain flour, for dusting
salt and pepper
oil for deep-frying
10 sticks spaghetti
75g lean smoked bacon, fine
julienne, no fat
2 litres good fish stock
small pinch of saffron threads
200g fennel, fine julienne
50g baby fennel stalks, finely sliced
75g carrot, fine julienne
75g white onion, fine julienne
75g red onion, fine julienne
75g celery, fine julienne
75g leek, fine julienne
75g spring onions, very finely sliced
for the herb salad
15g each of:
dill, chervil, tarragon,
coriander, flat-leaf parsley,
chives and red basil,
all picked very fine

Seafood broth

with lentils and beans, saffron and fennel, cockles,
mussels and lemon herb stew

For the pulses: blanch haricot beans and lentils separately. Prepare 4 pans, each with 10g sautéed mirepoix, 5g garlic, 20g poitrine, 1 bay leaf, 2 sprigs of thyme and 10g butter. Cover with chicken stock. Simmer for 35–45 minutes until cooked, leaving a little bite.

For the seafood: cut fish into small strips and wash under cold water. Steam open cockles and mussels and take out meat.

Separate calamari legs from body.

Cut calamari body into fine rings. Dust in flour, season and deep-fry.

Deep-fry 10 sticks of spaghetti and reserve.

Blanch smoked bacon julienne in fish stock with saffron, fennel and fennel stalks. Add fish (except Dover sole), slowly simmer for 2 minutes until all fish is cooked. Drop in cooked beans and lentils and warm through.

Steam Dover sole for 6 minutes over boiling water.

For the vegetables: mix all vegetables and add to steamer for further 1 minute.

To serve, position vegetables in centre of bowl and sit Dover sole on top. Arrange fish, beans and lentils neatly around vegetables. Arrange spaghetti in sole and thread calamari rings down spaghetti. Arrange herb salad on top of sole. Pour hot fish stock over all ingredients.

Haggis millefeuille

with bashed neeps and champit tatties, candied tomatoes, black pudding mousse, crisp rösti and malt whisky jus

for the candied tomatoes
4 plum tomatoes
25g sugar
5g sea salt
5g mixed herbs
1 clove of garlic, finely chopped

for the malt whisky jus
60g butter
50g chopped vegetables (e.g. carrot, leek, onion and celery)
60ml malt whisky
1 litre brown stock (beef or veal)
salt and pepper

for the crisp rösti
60ml olive oil
180g shredded raw potato
salt and pepper

for the black pudding mousse
300g black pudding
65g skinless chicken supreme (i.e. breast)

360g hot haggis
180g turnip purée
180g potato purée
25g leek, fine julienne, deep-fried

For the candied tomatoes: slice tomatoes and place in 4 interleaving circles approximately 10cm in diameter on an oven tray lined with silicone paper. Mix sugar, sea salt, mixed herbs and chopped garlic together. Sprinkle mixture evenly over circles of tomatoes. Place in preheated oven (150°C/gas mark 2) for 30 minutes. Remove and allow to cool.

For the malt whisky jus: melt half butter in thick-bottomed pan. Add chopped vegetables and cook gently for 2–3 minutes. Add malt whisky and flambé. Add brown stock and reduce by two-thirds. Remove from heat, season and whisk in remaining butter. Keep warm without boiling.

For the crisp rösti (12 rösti, 3 for each serving): heat olive oil in a small 10cm diameter saucepan. Season raw shredded potato with salt and pepper, and place a thin layer covering bottom of pan. Cook and colour rösti for few minutes then turn over with palette knife and colour other side. Repeat. If rösti needs more cooking place on roasting tray and finish cooking in a hot oven.

For the black pudding mousse: pass black pudding and chicken supreme through food processor for 4–5 minutes, making sure paste is smooth. Wrap mousse in clingfilm then in tinfoil to form a sausage shape. Secure with string. Steam over boiling water for 25 minutes until mousse is fully cooked. Reserve in hot place until assembly.

To serve, place a round pastry cutter in middle of serving plate and press a layer of haggis into the cutter. Place one of the rösti potatoes on top of haggis. Place one ring of candied tomatoes on rosti. Place pastry cutter on to tomato and press a layer of potato purée into cutter. Place another rösti potato and tomato ring on top of potato. Place pastry cutter on top of next tomato and press a layer of turnip into cutter. Place another rösti potato and tomato ring on top of turnip. Top tomato with black pudding mousse – your dish will be tower shaped. Drizzle malt whisky jus around plate and garnish with deep-fried leek.

Stewart Cameron
Turnberry Hotel

Medallion of Buccleuch beef

with wild forest mushrooms and baby asparagus, smoked artichokes, roast garlic cloves and truffled Madeira sauce

1 globe artichoke
juice of 1 lemon
5g garlic
50ml olive oil
salt and pepper
8 x 90g medallions Buccleuch beef fillet
75g butter
10g (total) chopped herbs (thyme, rosemary, tarragon and parsley)
12 cloves of garlic
10g shallots, finely chopped
90g mixed wild forest mushrooms
16 baby morel mushrooms
16 small bouchon ceps
24 spears baby asparagus
4 sprigs of chervil
4 sprigs of thyme
12 very fine slices of black truffle
for the truffled Madeira sauce
25g butter
75g (total) carrot, celery and onion, finely chopped
1 bay leaf
1g black peppercorns
160ml Madeira
1.5 litres rich beef stock
10g truffle, chopped

Blanch artichoke in boiling water with lemon juice to retain colour. Smoke over oak chippings for 1 hour or until artichokes are fully cooked. Trim off any excess outer leaves and, with a sharp knife, turn into a tart shape. Purée any artichoke trimmings with 5g garlic and spread evenly over artichoke.

Heat olive oil in a thick-bottomed pan until smoking. Season beef medallions and carefully place in pan, cooking to desired degree (rare, medium or well done). Remove medallions from pan and keep warm until needed to finish dish. Drain excess oil from pan.

Now make the sauce. Add butter and finely chopped vegetables, bay leaf and peppercorns. Cook gently for 1–2 minutes. Add Madeira and flambé. Add beef stock and reduce by two-thirds. Remove from heat and strain through muslin chinois. Add chopped truffle.

Melt 25g of butter in sauté pan. Add half chopped herbs to garlic and brown gently over direct heat. When nicely coloured, place in hot oven (190°C/gas mark 5) and finish cooking (9 minutes). Remove from oven and keep warm.

Melt 25g of butter in sauté pan. Add remaining chopped herbs and shallots to mushrooms, baby morels and ceps, and sauté quickly until cooked.

Blanch asparagus in boiling water and reserve.

To serve, arrange medallions in centre of large plate, layering wild mushrooms with baby ceps separately between two medallions. Arrange ceps, morels and wild mushrooms in half-moon shape with baby asparagus down left-hand side of plate. Arrange roast garlic evenly around plate. Position artichoke at top of plate with some mushrooms, asparagus, morels, chervil and thyme.

Return sauce to heat and bring quickly to the boil. Remove from heat and whisk remaining butter gently into sauce. Drizzle finished sauce over each of the plates, allowing a little of the sauce to cover one side of medallions. Arrange sliced truffle on top.

Stewart Cameron
Turnberry Hotel

Bitter chocolate mousse

with red capsicum ice cream, sweet sherry and Grenadine jus

for the chocolate mousse
400ml whipping cream
340g bitter dark chocolate, chopped
3 drops vanilla essence

for the chocolate coating
280g dark chocolate
40ml vegetable oil

for the sauce anglaise
340ml double cream
500ml milk
1 vanilla pod
7 egg yolks
90g castor sugar
vanilla essence

for the red capsicum ice cream
(45 portions)
100g castor sugar
25g glucose
375g red capsicum, puréed
1 litre sauce anglaise

for the sweet sherry and Grenadine jus
40g sugar
20ml water
40ml sweet sherry
12ml Grenadine

for the green pulled sugar
1kg granulated sugar
500ml water
200g glucose
8 drops tartaric acid
1/4 tsp green powder colour
a little melted dark chocolate for piping on plate

For the chocolate mousse: mix half cream and vanilla essence. Boil mixture and pour on to chopped chocolate and stir with wooden spoon until melted. Leave to cool slightly.

Whip remaining half of cream and fold into chocolate mix. Pour into silicone paper cornet (5.5cm diameter base x 10cm height). To support paper cornet, place in container of flour. Freeze for 24 hours.

Melt chocolate for coating and mix in vegetable oil (70g chocolate, 10ml oil per portion).

Take mousse out of freezer and remove paper. Place on cooling wire and, with a small ladle, coat mousse with chocolate coating. Remove from cooling wire and place on a piece of paper and put in fridge.

For the sauce anglaise: place cream, milk and vanilla pod in a pan and bring to the boil slowly.

Put egg yolks, sugar and vanilla essence in a bowl and whisk together well. Add half boiling liquid to eggs and sugar and place back on stove. Add the egg and sugar mixture to other boiling cream and milk. When sauce is ready it will coat back of spoon. Sieve into clean container and cool (so as not to curdle it).

For the red capsicum ice cream: dissolve sugar with glucose and a little of red capsicum purée in a pan over a medium heat, then add remaining purée. Add purée mix to sauce anglaise and put into ice-cream machine and churn for 8–12 minutes. Be careful not to over-churn. Put mixture into container. Freeze for 24 hours.

For the sweet sherry and Grenadine jus: bring sugar and water to the boil and wash down sides of pan with water. Add sweet sherry and Grenadine and bring to boil again. Boil to 106°C and then leave to cool.

For the green pulled sugar: bring to the boil in a copper pan (preferably) the sugar and wash down side of pan with water. Add glucose and when it comes back to boil wash down side again. Boil to 145°C and add tartaric acid. Mix green powder with a little water and add colour when liquid at 148°C. When sugar reaches 154°C take off heat and plunge pan into ice-cold water to stop cooking. Pour sugar on to oiled work surface or Silpat mat. When edges of sugar cool put it into centre and repeat until cool enough to pull sugar with your fingers.

Pull until it gives a shine. Pull length of 17cm. Bring top to a point leaving base 1cm in width, and mould over an oiled 11cm diameter pipe mould for a few minutes to set (5 pieces per portion). Pipe melted chocolate on to plate using a small cornet (see photo). Pipe sherry and Grenadine jus into chocolate design.

Ball ice cream with 2.5cm parisienne scoop and place back in freezer (5 balls per portion). Place sugar curves under mousse, leaving a little of wide base out to place ice cream on. Place ice cream balls one on each of sugar bases.

Serve.

Alan Craigie
The Creel

I've always enjoyed home baking and cooking. When I left school, I became an apprentice baker in Kirkwall, but knew I wanted to be a chef. At the end of the four years, I went to Telford College in Edinburgh and then stayed on, working at Prestonfield House and for Gardiner Merchant. Joyce and I had been going out before I left Orkney, and she came to join me in Edinburgh working as a nurse. We got a great job together in Los Angeles, working as chef and housekeeper for the British Consul. We came back to Orkney for a holiday and heard about the Creel – it had been a restaurant, but abandoned for three years.

We opened the Creel in 1985 and, for the first five years here, we lived above the restaurant. Then the Bank of Scotland next door closed down which we bought and made into our home. We then converted the upstairs of the Creel to rooms. This made a huge difference to our business. Before, people would come to Orkney for a holiday and eat with us maybe twice but, when they could stay, they would eat here every day for a week or more!

When we are open it's seven days a week, and we never really stop. We open from March to mid-October, and in December. Out of season is the time for renovation, for spending more time with our family, catching up with friends and walking. We also like to visit restaurants throughout Scotland during this time – we love trying other chef's cooking. We have a great life here by the sea. We want to keep trying to improve and maintain standards, but not really to expand.

Our food is as simple as possible, simply cooked and presented. We want the raw ingredients to speak for themselves. Our fish, shellfish, beef and vegetables are all sourced locally. We have just completed a small extension to the restaurant, providing a new reception area and breakfast room. The basic look of the restaurant hasn't changed at all – we have kept to the same friendly style, with paintings by local artists covering the walls. We want people to come here and enjoy the food in a relaxed, informal atmosphere.

Alan Craigie
The Creel

Fillet of beef

with onion marmalade, served with black pudding

for the onion marmalade

1 litre beef stock
600g sliced onions
5 cloves of garlic, sliced
2 tbsp olive oil
225ml white wine
4 tbsp balsamic vinegar
1 dessertspoon of fresh ginger, cut into thin strips
1 tbsp soft dark brown sugar
salt and pepper
black pudding (available from all good butchers)
fresh parsley

Reduce beef stock by half.

Sweat onion and garlic in olive oil in a covered pan until very soft. Remove lid and cook till golden brown. Add white wine, balsamic vinegar, ginger and sugar and gently cook to a thick syrup. Add the reduced stock; bring to a gentle simmer, taste and season with salt and pepper. Sprinkle in parsley and mix well.

Warm black pudding in a moderate oven, slice and place around the plate.

Serve with fillet of beef grilled to your taste.

Alan Craigie
The Creel

Green crab bisque

with chunks of fresh ling

50g butter
160g onion, chopped
160g leeks, chopped
160g celery, chopped
160g carrot, chopped
5 cloves of garlic, chopped
100ml white wine
400g tin of chopped tomatoes
1kg cooked and shelled velvet crab
2 litres fish stock
450g ling cut into 1cm chunks (any other white fish can be used if ling is not available)
50ml double cream
25g fresh parsley, chopped
salt and freshly milled pepper

for the beremeal bannocks

225g beremeal
225g plain flour
2 tsp bicarbonate of soda
1 tsp cream of tartar
50g butter
2 tbsp natural yoghurt, made up to 425ml with milk
1 egg

Melt butter in a large thick-bottomed pan and sweat onion, leek, celery, carrot and garlic (without colouring) until soft. Deglaze pan with wine, add chopped tomatoes and cook slowly until well reduced.

Add crabs and stock and gently simmer for around 1½ hours, topping up with stock if required.

Blend bisque with a heavy-duty blender until smooth. Pass through a conical strainer, pushing as much liquid as possible through with a wooden spoon, then pass through a fine strainer.

Put soup in a clean pan, bring to the boil and add chunks of ling. Simmer for 3–4 minutes, add double cream and chopped parsley and season to taste.

(Green crabs or shore crabs are fairly soft-shelled and will blend quite easily; as an alternative they could be pulverized with a rolling pin.)

Serve with beremeal bannocks.

For the beremeal bannocks: put all dry ingredients in Robot Coup, blend with butter until well mixed.

Mix together yoghurt, milk and egg.

Put dry bannock mix in a large bowl and make a well in the centre.

Pour most of milk, yoghurt and egg mixture into the well and mix with a fork.

Add the remainder if required (the mixture should be soft but not too sloppy).

This mixture will make 6 bannocks.

Cook them on a moderate griddle for 3–4 minutes on each side.

Roasted wolf-fish and skate wings

served with a cassoulet of cannellini beans

2 red peppers
4 tbsp olive oil
160g onion, chopped
160g celeriac, cut into thin strips
160g leeks
3 cloves of garlic, chopped
100ml white wine
420g tin of cannellini beans
4 tomatoes, skinned, deseeded and sliced
150ml double cream
25g fresh parsley
50g fresh basil
salt and pepper
500g each of wolf-fish and skate

Place red peppers in a small roasting tin and cook for 30–40 minutes at 190°C/gas mark 5 turning 2–3 times. When skins are well blistered remove from oven, cover with clingfilm and leave until cold.

Pour 1 tablespoon of olive oil into a thick-bottomed pan, place over a low heat, add onion, celeriac, leeks and garlic, cover with a lid and sweat over a low heat for 10 minutes. Deglaze pan with white wine and reduce to a glace. Strain liquid from beans and add them to the vegetables. Add tomatoes and reduce by half. Peel red peppers and remove seeds, put flesh into a blender and blend to a fine purée. Add purée to pan of vegetables and bring to a gentle simmer. Add cream and freshly chopped parsley and basil. Season with salt and pepper. Keep cassoulet warm for serving.

Roast wolf-fish and skate wings in the remaining olive oil in a hot non-stick pan in a moderate oven (175°C /gas mark 4) for 5–10 minutes until golden brown, depending on the thickness of the fillets and size of the skate wings.

Arrange neatly on a plate, serve with cassoulet and enjoy.

Alan Craigie
The Creel

Strawberry shortcake

for the shortbread
240g butter
120g castor sugar
270g plain flour
90g cornflour

for the custard
4 egg yolks
60g castor sugar
I vanilla pod
600ml double cream
icing sugar
300ml double cream
200g strawberries

For the shortbread: cream together butter and sugar, add flour and cornflour, mix gently into a dough, then roll out carefully and cut into shapes. Place shapes on to a greased and lightly floured baking tray and then chill for 30 minutes.

Place in a preheated oven (150–175°C/gas mark 2–4) and bake for 25–30 minutes.

Take out when golden brown and leave to cool. Store in airtight container.

For the custard: cream egg yolks and sugar in a large bowl.

Place vanilla pod and cream in a thick-bottomed pan and bring to a gentle simmer. Remove vanilla pod and whisk cream with eggs and sugar. Return custard mixture to a clean thick-bottomed pan and place over a low heat. Cook custard, stirring with a wooden spoon until it begins to coat the back of the spoon. Once custard has reached the correct consistency pour into a clean container and allow to cool.

It is most important that the custard does not boil as this will result in it curdling.

To finish, douse shortbread with icing sugar, heat a skewer over an open gas flame and brand shortbread.

Lightly whip cream. Layer shortbread with sliced strawberries and cream, placing the branded shortbread biscuit on top.

Flood plate with cold custard, place shortcake in the centre of the plate and garnish with remainder of the strawberries.

Lesley Crosfield and Colin Craig
The Albannach

Lesley: I went to Art School, but always loved cooking for my friends. I was running a hotel in the Trossachs when I met Colin and we decided to look for a place of our own. The search took two years, but then we found this house overlooking Lochinver and knew this was it. That was more than eleven years ago and we love it and what we do.

Colin: I studied Geology at University and was a manager in an electronics factory in Livingston when I met Lesley. Well, in fact, I was drowning my sorrows when I met her and she thought I was glaring at her all evening! Much to my surprise, she invited me back for Hogmanay – I turned up with a group of friends, and the band that was supposed to play didn't arrive, so we sang and played and generally made ourselves useful!

Lesley: We both cook, which surprises people because Colin presents the food too – in his kilt! My bible is 'Mastering the Art of French Cooking', a two-volume cookery book I was given at twenty-five. I've learned all the basics from it, but over the years I've honed and pared, leaving behind the more old-fashioned, heavy and creamy style of cooking.

Colin: I always enjoyed eating out and was aware of the enviable produce that Scotland can offer a well-placed rural chef. At the Albannach we've always used local, fresh ingredients. We won't use anything unless it's free-range or wild. I hand-dive for scallops when I have time, and a friend's creels supply us with crabs and lobsters, crayfish and langoustines.

Lesley: Over the years we've become more and more interested in food and in improving what we can cook for our guests. Our ambitions with the food made us realise we had to improve the rooms. We keep adding extensions and planning improvements to the place, not to get more people in necessarily, just to make more of the space. Colin's just bought the croft next door and we've got plans for poly-tunnels!

Lesley Crosfield and Colin Craig
The Albannach

Roast fillet of hill-fed Highland lamb

on Puy lentils, with port and rosemary sauce, celeriac tartlet and kale 'n' pine nuts

approximately 900g Morayshire lamb saddle, boned to the eye
3 tbsp hazelnut oil

for the sauce
2 tbsp brandy
150ml port
570ml strong, dark lamb stock
50g butter
1 sprig of rosemary

kale 'n' pine nuts
1 head of curly kale
1 tbsp each raisins (soaked in boiling water and drained) and pine nuts
1 clove of garlic, mashed
1 tbsp olive oil

celeriac tartlets
1 small head of celeriac
4 x 5cm pastry tartlet cases (pre-baked)
50g unsalted butter
2 tbsp water
sea salt and freshly ground black pepper
1 tbsp double cream
a squeeze of lemon

Puy lentils
4 tbsp Puy lentils
salt
1 tsp fennel seeds (optional)
1 clove of garlic, mashed
1 tbsp olive oil
1 tsp balsamic vinegar
1 tbsp fresh coriander leaves, chopped

Trim lamb fillet of all skin, fat and membrane. This should leave 680–800g trimmed weight. Cut it into 4 lengths approximately 175–200g each. Place in a dish, turn in the hazelnut oil, cover and refrigerate (preferably overnight, but for at least 7 hours). Remove from the fridge 1 hour before cooking.

For the sauce: rapidly reduce brandy in a small, heavy saucepan until sticky. Add port, and reduce rapidly again until slightly caramelised. Add hot lamb stock gradually. Whisk in small pieces of butter and reduce by half. Infuse with rosemary. Set aside and keep warm.

Trim away the tough stems of kale and steam for 3 minutes. It should still be bright green but limp. Refresh in cold water, pat dry and roughly chop. In a large pan sauté garlic, raisins and pine nuts in the olive oil until pine nuts are golden. Add kale and stir together over a low heat for 2 minutes. Remove to a ceramic dish and set aside.

Peel and cut celeriac into 0.5cm cubes, like a swede. Cook it in the butter, water, salt and pepper, covered, until very soft and the water is gone. Process with cream and lemon juice. Return to saucepan and reserve, warm.

Boil lentils in salted water with fennel seeds and garlic in a covered saucepan until tender. Drain and add olive oil, balsamic vinegar and coriander. Keep this warm.

Preheat over to 230°C/gas mark 8. Preheat buttered baking tray for 5 minutes before roasting weighed lamb fillet pieces. Calculate the cooking time as 1 minute per 25g plus 2 minutes (i.e. for 175-200g piece, 9-10 minutes).

Remove from oven and cover with foil to rest meat while finishing the dish.

Reheat tartlet cases in the switched-off oven. Briefly reheat kale dish (microwave is best). Slice each fillet piece diagonally in 4 and arrange on warm plates, propped against a small pile of lentils, a tartlet filled with celeriac purée to one side, a small pile of kale 'n' pine nuts, and the sauce alongside the meat.

Hand-dived, Loch Broom scallops and roasted monkfish tails

with saffron and seaweed rice and Vermouth sabayon

1 monkfish tail approximately 800g
sea salt
ground black pepper
1 tbsp fresh thyme, stalks removed,
and rolled flat to release aroma
2 tbsp olive oil
8 scallops
1 clove of garlic, mashed
1 tbsp hazelnut oil
50g melted, clarified, unsalted
butter
½ lemon, squeezed

for the saffron and seaweed rice
845ml vegetable stock
big pinch of saffron fronds
3 leaves dried Kombu Japanese
seaweed
1 fennel bulb, diced
1 stalk of celery, diced
1 tbsp olive oil
25g unsalted butter
1 cup basmati rice
75ml dry vermouth
1 clove of garlic, mashed
small pinch of cayenne
1 tbsp flat-leaf parsley, chopped

Using a flexible, thin-bladed knife, slice down either side of monkfish backbone, leaving two tapering fillets. (The backbone and any trimmings make an excellent stock for the vermouth sabayon.)

Carefully slice away the inelegant, thin membrane which covers monkfish tail like a slimy glove, to reveal the firm white meat. This should leave 550–700g of fillet. Cut each fillet into two equal pieces, approximately 150–200g each.

Place fillets side by side in a ceramic dish, sprinkle with sea salt, black pepper and thyme. Turn in olive oil and refrigerate until 1 hour before cooking.

Having removed scallops from their shells and discarded the 'skirts', leaving only the white meat and orange roe, place them in a plastic or ceramic container and grind black pepper over them. Turn them in the mashed garlic and refrigerate until 10 minutes before cooking.

For the saffron and seaweed rice: boil stock and pour it over saffron and whole leaves of seaweed. Leave to soak for 10 minutes. A large, heat-resistant jug is ideal for this, as you will be pouring this brew on to the rice a little at a time. Remove seaweed and chop finely.

In a heavy-bottomed saucepan, sweat fennel and celery in oil and butter, lid on. When soft, add seaweed and slowly cook, lid on, for a further 5 minutes.

Add rice and turn up the heat, stirring to coat rice and prevent it from sticking, and cook until a nutty smell and slight brittleness tells you it's time to add liquid (about 5 minutes). Add vermouth, garlic and cayenne, boil liquid away and start adding ladlefuls (approximately if pouring from a jug) of seaweed and saffron-flavoured vegetable stock, stirring vigorously all the while to aid absorption and prevent sticking. Let each ladleful of stock be absorbed before adding the next.

After 20 minutes or so, test rice is cooked by eating a bit. If it's still chewy, stir in a half-ladle of boiling water and, while still quite wet, switch off heat and cover. Leave for 15 minutes. Stir and fork through chopped parsley (coriander may be substituted if rice is accompanying a more exotic dish). Turn into an open, ceramic dish, cover with foil and reheat in a moderate oven when required. This is a very tolerant dish as risotto variants go, and can even be microwaved uncovered, for extra separate fluffiness after being in oven.

for the vermouth sabayon

3 shallots, finely chopped
25g unsalted butter
75ml dry vermouth
150ml dry white wine
300ml fish stock
330ml double cream
3 egg yolks
2 tbsp warm clarified butter
sea salt
white pepper

For the vermouth sabayon: sweat the shallots in the unsalted butter until soft and translucent. Add vermouth and wine and boil down to a syrup. Add fish stock and reduce by half. Add cream and cook until it coats the back of a spoon (about 5 minutes). Cool slightly.

Meanwhile cook egg yolks with a few drops of cold water, whisking over a pan of hot water until pale and thick. Remove from heat, whisk in clarified butter; add this to strained cream sauce.

Continue gentle cooking over hot water until thick pouring consistency is achieved. Season gently with sea salt and white pepper. Keep this warm. To finish, sear monkfish in hazelnut oil for 2 minutes on each side before transferring it to a preheated baking tray and roasting for 4 minutes at 230°C/gas mark 8. Meanwhile sear scallops in clarified butter, sprinkling with sea salt and lemon juice, in a very hot, heavy frying pan, 2 minutes on each side or until nicely caramelised but not at all overcooked.

To serve, press a portion of rice into centrally placed mousse rings on 4 warm plates; remove rings; carve each piece of monkfish into 3 large, flattish escalopes and arrange them on rice with 2 scallops atop. Surround with velvety sabayon.

The best accompaniments would be brightly coloured, fresh-tasting vegetables such as aubergine-stuffed tomatoes and roasted whole yellow courgettes, or asparagus spears and roasted red peppers.

Roast red pepper soufflé
with red onion marmalade

for the onion marmalade

700g red onions
40g unsalted butter
75g demerara sugar
1 $\frac{1}{2}$ tbsp crème de cassis
2 $\frac{1}{2}$ tbsp sherry vinegar
2 tsp salt

for the red pepper soufflé

50g unsalted butter, plus extra for
greasing
40g plain flour
110ml milk
slice of onion or $\frac{1}{2}$ shallot
275g red peppers, roasted,
skinned and seeded
1 tsp tomato juice
1 tsp lemon juice
white pepper
50g grated Parmesan (Reggiano)
2 free-range egg yolks
3 egg whites at room temperature
sea salt
cream of tartare

For the onion marmalade: peel and finely slice onions, melt butter in a heavy-bottomed pan and sweat onions gently until softened but not coloured. Add the other ingredients and cook, uncovered on a low heat, stirring occassionally for about 90 minutes, to a moist and soft, not dry, marmalade. Cool and reserve.

For the soufflés: butter 4 ramekins and chill. Melt butter in heavy-bottomed pan and gently cook flour until there is a nutty smell. Set aside. Warm milk gently with onion or shallot and allow to infuse for 15 minutes off the heat. Chop peppers roughly, then purée in food processor, adding tomato juice and lemon juice. Warm butter and flour mixture then remove from the heat and add strained milk, then pepper purée, stirring constantly. Add a little white pepper to taste, if required.

Cook over a low heat, stirring regularly for about 40 minutes, when texture should be noticeably lighter.

Place grated Parmesan in heatproof glass bowl and add pepper mixture; fold together until cheese is amalgamated. Cool. Beat egg yolks and add to pepper mixture.

Beat egg whites until frothy then add pinch of salt and pinch of cream of tartare. Continue to beat until firm peaks form.

Blend $\frac{1}{2}$ egg white (with whisk) into pepper mix then with a spatula fold in remainder. Fill ramekins, smoothing top with a palette knife. Loosen mixture from side of ramekin with the point of a knife.

Cook for 25 minutes in a roasting tray filled with boiling water to two-thirds of the way up ramekins in an oven preheated to 190°C/gas mark 5. Soufflés should be well risen and slightly browned.

Serve immediately with a spoonful of tepid marmalade alongside. Any marmalade remaining will keep in refrigerator in a sealed jar for about 2 weeks.

Lesley Crosfield and Colin Craig
The Albannach

Lime torte

with berry baskets and three sauces

for the sponge

3–4 free-range eggs
200g castor sugar
110g self-raising flour
1 tsp cornflour
40g unsalted butter
4 tbsp water
1 tsp baking powder
icing sugar

For the sponge: preheat oven to 200°C/gas mark 6. Beat the eggs in free-standing mixer until well risen then gradually add sugar, continuing to beat at high speed until colour and texture are light. Fold in flour and cornflour (sifted). Bring butter and water to the boil. Sieve baking powder into egg and flour mixture then pour over the boiling butter. After a few seconds fold in carefully. Pour mixture into tray and level with spatula. Bake for about 15 minutes until well risen and golden, springing to the touch. Cool on wire tray and set aside.

for the almond tuille baskets

150g unsalted butter
150g castor sugar
2 free-range eggs, beaten
10g flour
150g finely ground almonds

for the lime filling

$1/2$ gelatine leaf
110g Mascarpone or similar
50g castor sugar
2 eggs, separated
110ml double cream
juice and zest of $1 1/2$ limes
cream of tartare

for the lemon/orange caramel

200g castor sugar
150ml lemon and orange juice
(half each)

for the honey and lime sauce

juice of 2 limes, zest of 1 lime
2 tbsp heather honey
110ml sorbet syrup

for the berry coulis

110g fruit purée – strawberry,
raspberry, brambles, etc
55ml sorbet syrup

for the sorbet syrup

50g castor sugar, 75ml water
25ml liquid glucose
(store in fridge)

berry fruits

best seasonally available are
redcurrants, raspberries,
blueberries, brambles,
strawberries etc

equipment

60 x 30cm baking tray, buttered/
lined with buttered Silpat
4 x 7cm stainless-steel mousse
rings
4 egg cups, lightly greased with
flavourless oil

For the almond tuille baskets: cream butter and sugar in a bowl. Incorporate egg a little at a time, then flour, then almonds, until mixed thoroughly, and chill overnight.

Using a thin template, spread 4 x 7cm circles on a baking sheet lined with Silpat. Bake at 160°C/gas mark 3 for about 15 minutes until the edges are light brown.

Lift from sheet and bend over upturned egg cups to form baskets. Remove carefully and store in airtight container.

For the lime filling: cut 4 x 7cm discs from sponge. Slice each across the middle and place lower half at bottom of mousse rings on a baking tray set. Set aside tops while making the filling.

Soak gelatine in cold water for several minutes. Blend Mascarpone, half the sugar and the egg yolks in a processor (or free-standing mixer) add cream (with motor running) then lime zest.

Squeeze out gelatine and warm with lime juice until melted, then blend into Mascarpone mixture.

Whisk egg whites until frothy, then add a pinch of cream of tartare. Continue whisking at high speed, adding remaining sugar gradually until soft peaks form.

Fold carefully into Mascarpone. Fill mousse rings to just below the top, then carefully place top of sponge discs on top. Chill for 2 hours minimum (will keep overnight).

For the lemon/orange caramel: heat sugar slowly in heavy-bottomed pan until pale caramel; meanwhile heat and strain fruit juice. Remove caramel from heat and add hot juice, stirring with a long-handled spoon. Return to heat and cook slowly, stirring constantly until sugar is dissolved. Strain and reserve. Once caramel has cooled, refrigerate (keeps indefinitely).

For the honey and lime sauce: mix all ingredients together and chill.

For the berry coulis: purée fruit with sorbet syrup, strain and chill.

For the sorbet syrup: heat ingredients in a pan for about 5 minutes (do not allow to colour).

To serve, dust tortes with icing sugar. Fill baskets with assorted berries. De-mould tortes onto white plate by running a thin knife round the inside of ring very carefully.

Place filled basket alongside and decorate with the three sauces (however it takes your fancy!) but use only a few drops of the honey and lime sauce which is rather strong.

Andrew Fairlie
Andrew Fairlie at Gleneagles

As a sixteen-year-old apprentice working in my home town of Perth, I dreamed of working in one of the great restaurants of France. Four years later – after completing my apprenticeship – I won the Roux scholarship and realised my dream. My prize took me to the kitchens of Michel Guerard in South West France. It was while working with Guerard that I learned an understanding of food and to respect the traditions of French cookery.

My inspiration and style of cuisine comes largely from the time I spent with Guerard and I cannot thank the Roux brothers enough for introducing me to one of the truly great chefs of the world.

I stayed in France for more than five years, working in Paris and the French Alps in the south. It was so easy to see why France is the most popular tourist destination in Europe. Clearly people are drawn to its diversity and to the standard of cooking.

As a country, Scotland has an abundance of superb produce. If I have a criticism it is that our profession does not fully exploit what we have on our doorstep. Perhaps if we did, tourism in Scotland would be in a generally healthier state.

I was Head Chef at One Devonshire Gardens in Glasgow for over six years and have just opened my own restaurant at Gleneagles. Although my style is very French, I use as much Scottish produce as I can. Over the years, I have built up strong relationships with small suppliers who feel as passionate about their produce as I do about my cooking. We really should support small suppliers because, ultimately, it is to all our benefit – quality ingredients are the key to great food.

On my last day with Michel Guerard he told me that I had chosen "a beautiful but all consuming profession", and he was right. I feel very privileged to have found such a creative, pleasure-giving pursuit that to this day still excites me as much as when I was a sixteen-year-old apprentice.

Baked scallops in their shells

100g carrot
30g fresh ginger
100g leek
100g endive
50g butter
1 tbsp redcurrant jelly
juice of 2 oranges
4 large scallops (in shell)
4 strips puff pastry
1 egg yolk
for the sauce
300ml orange juice
200ml fish stock
200ml double cream
100g butter, diced
salt and pepper

Cut all vegetables into fine juliennes. Melt butter in a saucepan, sweat vegetables until cooked but still crunchy – starting with carrot and ginger, then leeks and finally endive.

Boil redcurrant jelly and orange juice until syrupy and add to vegetables. Open scallops and remove scallop meat, discarding roe and skirt. Wash and pat dry.

Thoroughly scrub scallop shells and boil in water for 5 minutes, then refresh under cold water and dry.

Divide vegetable mixture between 4 shells. Heat a non-stick frying pan until very hot then sear scallops very quickly, just enough to colour meat. Once seared, place one scallop on to each pile of vegetables in shell.

Replace top half of shell. Brush strips of puff pastry with egg yolk and seal around each shell. Brush over again with egg yolk.

For the sauce: reduce orange juice and fish stock until syrupy consistency, then add cream. Boil, then whisk in cold diced butter, and season.

Place scallop shells in a preheated oven (200°C/gas mark 6) for 11 minutes for large shells and a little less for smaller shells.

To serve, pour rock salt on to 4 serving plates, place baked scallops on to each pile of salt and serve, keeping the sauce separate in a sauceboat.

Marrbury smoked salmon

with scrambled eggs, herb salad and avruga caviar

200g untrimmed Marrbury
smoked salmon

for the mousse

100g (of 200g) salmon trimmings
10g butter
1½ sheets of gelatine, soaked
100ml fish stock
splash of tabasco sauce
splash of Worcestershire sauce
150ml cream, whipped

for the scrambled eggs

4 eggs
30g unsalted butter
100ml double cream
1 shallot, chopped
1 bunch of chives, chopped

for the herb salad

flat-leaf parsley, tarragon, chervil,
dill, chives
few drops of lemon juice
few drops of olive oil
salt and pepper
avruga caviar, to garnish

Purée trimmings off side of salmon and mix with butter. Melt gelatine in fish stock. Mix salmon purée, gelatine/stock mix, tabasco and Worcestershire sauce in mixer. Pass through sieve and fold in whipped cream.

For the roulade: slice a side of smoked salmon very thinly and lay it out on a sheet of clingfilm longways, then season with salt and pepper. Pipe mousse along bottom of salmon, then roll salmon into thin roulade. Tie roulade at both ends and put in fridge to set. Once set, cut into two nice batons.

For the scrambled eggs: whisk eggs together. Melt butter in pan and cook eggs gently on a low heat. Once eggs start to come together add double cream, shallot, chives and season.

Season herbs with a few drops of lemon juice, olive oil and salt and pepper. Garnish with avruga caviar.

Roast breast of grouse

with wild mushroom and potato pavé

4 grouse, legs and breast removed
2 pigeon breasts
300ml double cream
salt and pepper
500g pig's caul
1 tbsp olive oil
for the sauce
grouse carcass
4 shallots, chopped
2 carrots, chopped
$\frac{1}{2}$ leek, chopped
1 clove of garlic, chopped
400ml red wine
500ml chicken stock
1 sprig of thyme
1 bay leaf
**for the wild mushroom and
potato pavé**
4 large potatoes, peeled
250g butter
25g tarragon, parsley and chives,
chopped
500g mixed wild mushrooms
2 shallots, finely chopped
1 clove of garlic, crushed

Remove meat from grouse legs and blitz in a food processor with pigeon breasts. Put meat into a bowl, set over ice and gradually beat double cream into meat, then season with salt and pepper.

Divide pig's caul into 8 even-sized pieces, big enough to wrap each grouse breast fully. Lay out caul on table and spread a little of pigeon mixture on to it, then place a grouse breast on top. Lightly season and cover with more pigeon mousse then wrap caul around breasts to cover completely. Repeat with rest of breasts and keep refrigerated until ready to use.

For the sauce: chop grouse carcass and brown in a heavy saucepan, then add chopped vegetables and cook for 5 minutes. Add red wine and reduce by two-thirds, then add chicken stock and herbs and simmer gently for 45 minutes. Strain through a sieve and reduce by two-thirds, then check seasoning.

For the wild mushroom and potato pavé: trim 1 large potato into a thin cylinder shape and slice very thinly into discs. Grate remaining 3 potatoes, wash in cold water and squeeze out to dry. Melt 100g butter in heavy frying pan and quickly fry grated potato until translucent and soft, then mix in herbs, season and remove from heat. Heat 100g of butter in heavy pan and quickly sauté wild mushrooms and drain into colander. In same pan, sweat off shallots and garlic, then put mushrooms back into pan. Sauté together and season, then remove from heat. Heat remaining butter in small pan and add sliced potato discs. Heat gently until discs are soft but not cooked.

Place 4 rings (approximately 65mm diameter) on to a small baking tray and arrange potato discs into each ring. Fill rings with alternate layers of cooked mushrooms and cooked grated potato. Bake in a pre-heated oven at 190°C/gas mark 5 for 20 minutes, rest for 5 minutes and then turn upside down to serve.

Heat olive oil in a heavy bottomed frying pan and place grouse breasts into pan and gently brown on both sides. Place into a preheated oven at 190°C/gas mark 5 for 7–9 minutes then remove from oven and rest for 5 minutes.

To serve, place potato and mushroom pavé on top of warmed plate, slice grouse breast (2 per person) and lay on plate and pour hot sauce around.

Hot chocolate biscuit
with vanilla ice cream

200g cream
60ml water
50g butter
120g dark chocolate, chopped
for the chocolate biscuit
110g dark chocolate
50g butter
2 egg yolks
40g ground almonds
40g cornflour
2 egg whites
90g castor sugar
for the ice cream
4 vanilla pods
6 egg yolks
500ml milk
170g sugar
250ml double cream

Boil cream and water, melt butter into it, then whisk in chopped chocolate until smooth. Pour this mix into 4 x 40mm dariole moulds and freeze.

For the chocolate biscuit: melt chocolate and butter in a bowl over gently simmering pot of water.

Mix in yolks until smooth, then add ground almonds and cornflour.

Whisk egg whites and sugar until you have stiff peaky meringue and then fold into chocolate mix.

Double line 65mm dessert rings with parchment paper. Pipe in approximately 2.5cm of pudding mix and place frozen chocolate de-moulded into centre. Pipe rest of biscuit mix around and over frozen centre then freeze. Bake when required in oven at 180°C/gas mark 4, for approximately 25 minutes.

For ice cream: split and scrape vanilla pods and add seeds to yolks. Boil milk and scraped pods and infuse for 25 minutes. Whisk yolks, seeds and sugar until double in volume and white. Pour one quarter of milk on to yolks and mix well. Add yolk mixture to milk and cook gently on a medium to low heat, until mixture coats back of spoon. Do not boil.

Remove from heat and add double cream, chill overnight, then turn in an ice-cream machine.

Ian Ferguson and Stephen Steele
Brig O'Doon

Ian: I've always loved cooking, since I was knee-high and helped my mum in the kitchen, doing the baking – I used to love licking the bowl. At fifteen, I went to college in Kirkcaldy and then went on to work at the Stakis Dunblane Hydro. The chefs used to fight over who would take the Sunday roast to Sir Reo Stakis, who lived in a house in the grounds – Sir Reo used to give a good tip! After five years at Dunblane I moved to Lochgreen House Hotel and worked my way up to become senior sous chef. When Costley & Costley opened Brig O'Doon, I went to set up the kitchen and have been Head Chef here ever since.

Stephen: I never thought of being anything other than a chef. I did a bit of cooking at school, but it was my gran who inspired me – she was a cook and very good at baking. I've been at Brig O'Doon for nearly two years and I love it. I love creating my own dishes and seeing people enjoy them. I'm learning loads from Ian about cooking and quality, and maintaining standards for the hundreds of lunches and dinners we cook, seven days a week.

Ian: Brig O'Doon is a busy place; we get lots of tourists in the season, but also from all over the west coast. Weddings are a big part of our business – people love the setting (overlooking the Burns Monument), especially at night with all the lights. Brig O'Doon only has five bedrooms, but we have three kitchens: one for the restaurant, one for functions, and one for the busy coffee shop. Brig O'Doon food is about taste, quality and value for money. Working as a chef for Costley & Costley means using good quality produce (Scottish, as far as possible), working hard and coping well with pressure, and maintaining the highest standards of cooking and cleanliness. The restaurants are all in great locations and the kitchens are magnificent.

for the white wine sauce
75g shallot
25g unsalted butter
250cl white wine
250cl Noilly Prat
1 litre fish stock
500ml double cream
juice of ½ lemon

for the mornay sauce
50g butter
50g plain flour
300ml whole milk
1 onion, shredded
5g fresh nutmeg
100g strong Cheddar cheese, grated
salt and pepper

for the cod
700g salt cod
1litre milk
1 bouquet garni
250ml water

for the garlic and chive sauce
200g garlic, blanched
100g shallots, blanched
160g crème fraîche
200g double cream
500ml water
750ml white wine sauce
salt and pepper
50g chives

4 x 150g jacket potatoes
3g freshly ground nutmeg
500g leeks, blanched
500ml mornay sauce
8 slices Parma ham (round)
cracked black pepper

Stuffed baked potato
with cod, leeks, crisp Parma ham and a garlic and chive sauce

For the white wine sauce: sweat off shallots with the butter.
Add and reduce white wine by two-thirds.
Add and reduce Noilly Prat by two-thirds.
Add fish stock, reduce by half.
Add cream and squeeze of lemon juice.
Strain.

For the mornay sauce: melt butter and add the flour slowly and mix well until it forms a roux.
Warm the milk with the shredded onion and nutmeg and add a ladle at a time to the roux over a low heat. Mix well.
Leave on a low heat and cook for 12-15 minutes.
Then add the grated Cheddar and season.

For the cod: place salt cod in cold water and leave for 24 hours.
Drain and poach in milk with bouquet garni and 250ml water for 10 minutes or until flesh becomes flaky. When cool, flake and remove bones.

For the garlic and chive sauce: place garlic, shallot, crème fraîche and double cream in remaining water, simmer for 30 minutes. Then blend in mixer. Whisk in white wine sauce and bring to the boil. Season to taste. Add chives before serving.

Wash potatoes, wrap in tinfoil and bake in the oven for 45 minutes until soft.
Cut potato lengthways. Scoop out flesh, leaving 0.5cm from the skin.
Place potato skins in the fryer for 10 minutes at 160°C to crispen. Season with nutmeg.
Slice leeks finely, add to mornay sauce (see above), along with cod and half the garlic and chive sauce . Warm through.
Grill Parma ham until crispy. Allow to cool.
Spoon mixture into the potato skins, top with crisp Parma ham, cracked black pepper and serve with remaining garlic cream.

Ian Ferguson and Stephen Steele
Brig O'Doon

Lightly curried selection of seafood

served with Charentais melon, lemon grass and coriander

for the nage

2 onions, coarsely chopped
2 leeks, coarsely chopped
2 celery stalks, coarsely chopped
1 whole head of garlic, sliced horizontally
6 lemon slices
8 white peppercorns
20 coriander seeds
1 bay leaf
2 star anise
pinch of saffron strands
8 sticks of lemon grass
1/2 red chilli
1.5 litres fish stock
1 sprig of coriander
1 sprig of thyme
1 sprig of parsley
200ml white wine
Flesh of 4 Charentais melons

for the saffron potatoes

12 potatoes
500ml fish stock
20ml white wine
2 shallots, finely diced
pinch of saffron
salt and pepper

200g salmon
200g red mullet
200g halibut
200g turbot
500g Shetland mussels, shelled
25g cumin
25g coriander
10g saffron sprigs
25g medium-hot curry powder
salt and pepper
8 langoustines
12 asparagus tips, blanched
1 sprig of fresh coriander, chopped
Charentais melon, diced

For the nage: place all the ingredients (except fish stock, fresh herbs, white wine and Charentais melon flesh) in a large pan. Cover with fish stock and bring to the boil. Simmer for 8-10 minutes.

Remove from the heat and add fresh herbs, white wine and Charentais melon. Leave to rest for approximately 2 hours in a warm place to infuse. Pass through a fine sieve (coffee filters are ideal).

Keep in a container in fridge. This will keep for 2-3 days.

For the saffron potatoes: cut potatoes into barrel shapes. Cook in mixture of fish stock and white wine, with shallots, pinch of saffron and salt and pepper.

Cut all the fish (except langoustines) into bite-size pieces and dust with dried cumin and coriander, sprinkle with saffron sprigs, white wine and a little curry powder. Season.

Steam coated fish with langoustines for 2-3 minutes until cooked.

Heat fish nage, add saffron potatoes, asparagus and warm through.

To serve, add fresh chopped coriander and diced Charentais melon to nage.

Coat fish with nage and arrange saffron potatoes and asparagus around the dish.

Ian Ferguson and Stephen Steele
Brig O'Doon

Ballotine of wild game
served with cider fondant potato and seared foie gras

for the red wine jus
3 shallots, finely sliced
3 cloves of garlic
4 sprigs of thyme
5g brown sugar
50ml red wine
50ml port
1 litre veal stock
25g butter, diced

for the ballotine
100g Puy lentils
4 breasts of guinea fowl
1 medium carrot (diced)
4 breasts of woodland pigeon
half small celeriac
400g venison fillets
1 medium leek
500g baby spinach leaves, blanched
100ml double cream
50g parsley coarsely chopped
2 eggs
salt and pepper
100g pistachio nuts, skinned
4 slices of fresh foie gras
4 potatoes square cut
100g prunes, stoned
200ml cider (Scrumpy Jack)
100g dried apricots, soaked in brandy
250g butter
1 red pepper, diced
100ml virgin olive oil
juice of 1 lemon
50ml white wine vinegar
50ml balsamic vinegar

For the red wine jus: sweat off shallots, garlic and thyme. Sprinkle brown sugar over to caramelise. Deglaze with red wine. Reduce. Add port and veal stock and bring to the boil. Simmer for 20 minutes, skimming frequently. Sieve through fine muslin. Whisk in chilled butter.

For the ballotine: trim all meat of excess fat. Bat out guinea fowl breasts and lay on a sheet of clingfilm.

Lay blanched baby spinach leaves on to guinea fowl breasts and place in fridge, allowing spinach to cool.

Make venison mousse by blending venison flesh with a little of the cream and pass through a fine mesh sieve. Cool in fridge. Add remainder of the cream and eggs slowly until well incorporated. Season and leave to rest.

Cut pigeon breasts into strips of 1cm thickness.

Into venison mousse fold pistachio nuts, prunes, apricots and diced red pepper.

Smooth mousse on to guinea fowl breasts and place pigeon strips in the centre.

Roll breasts, using the clingfilm, into a tight sausage shape and tie the ends of the clingfilm.

Wrap in tinfoil and poach in simmering water for about 45-50 minutes. Leave to rest.

Cook lentils in boiling salted water for about 15 minutes, drain and season.

Dice carrot, celeriac and leek and fry in a little olive oil until lightly brown. Add lentils.

Make vinaigrette by whisking together olive oil, balsamic vinegar, white wine vinegar and lemon juice. Season. Add to lentils and finish with the chopped parsley.

Brown all the edges of potato in 250g butter and add cider with a little water and finish fondant in an oven at 180°C/gas mark 4 for 8-10 minutes.

Season foie gras and fry in a hot pan with no oil for approximately 30 seconds each side.

Slice ballotine into 1cm strips, warm through.

To serve, arrange lentils at the side of the plate, top with ballotine.

Place fondant on the plate with seared foie gras.

Drizzle with red wine jus.

Ian Ferguson and Stephen Steele
Brig O'Doon

Thin tart of seared strawberries

with black pepper and ginger beer sorbet

for the tart

80g sugar

170g butter

1 small egg

250g flour

for the custard filling

60g strawberries

5g cornflour

1 egg yolk

25g sugar

for the garnish

200g sugar

100ml water

25ml fraise liquor

6 medium strawberries per tart

4 sprigs of mint

for the sorbet

100ml stock syrup

(made with 50ml water and 50g

castor sugar, boiled together)

300ml ginger beer

10g black pepper

50ml water

For the tart: gently cream sugar with butter. Add egg. Fold in flour. Roll out as thin as you dare and bake blind at 180°C/gas mark 4.

For the custard filling: purée the strawberries and strain. Boil purée and thicken with cornflour and yolk. Add sugar and allow to cool. Half fill tart.

For the garnish: boil sugar and water to make stock syrup. Add liquor and pour over strawberries. Allow to cool.

For the sorbet: make heavy stock syrup. Combine all ingredients. Turn in ice-cream machine for 20 minutes. Place in shallow tray or tin and freeze.

To serve, warm tart gently and fill with custard – not too much. Build the berries up in the tart to garnish. Add mint and sorbet.

Peter Fleming
Cameron House

I started cooking when I was about twelve. I used to do an early-morning milk round and when I got home I was always starving, so I'd make myself something to eat. I come from Coatbridge in Lanarkshire – not a place that breeds many chefs! I started working in a kitchen, locally, at sixteen and then Ian Ross, a lecturer at Motherwell Food Tech helped me to get a job at Gleneagles. I was there for four years. It was hard work and, for two years, I seemed to spend most of my time cleaning. But I learned a lot about planning and discipline in the kitchen. After Gleneagles, I worked in restaurants all over the place, including the Channel Islands and Cheshire.

I believe in keeping things simple with food. "Honesty" is my favourite word where cooking is concerned. If you ran your own restaurant, I don't think you could make a living cooking the kind of food we serve here. Ingredients like foie gras, beef fillet, lobster, they don't come cheap, but people expect to find them on the menu. Quality control is so important to the job. That's the starting point for everything I try to do here: if the raw ingredients are good, you can't go far wrong. We try to make as much of the food as possible last minute, so that it's freshly prepared. And we concentrate on getting the basics right: newly baked bread at the start of a meal sets a standard for the rest of the food.

I've been here at Cameron House for nearly nine years now. These days, I'm in charge of all the food we serve in the hotel – the dishes I've chosen are from the Georgian Room, which is our Michelin starred restaurant, but we also have a larger brasserie-style restaurant, Smolletts. And then, of course, there's always room service and the canteen for our 200 staff. It all keeps me busy! It's great that there's a gym here – I try to spend an hour there every afternoon – it helps me to unwind as well as to keep on top of things.

Peter Fleming
Cameron House

Ravioli of scallop with red pesto

for the pasta
550g plain flour/soft wheat Italian flour
$\frac{1}{2}$ tsp fine sea salt
4 large eggs
6 egg yolks
2 tsp olive oil
1 egg yolk, for wash

for the pesto
2 red peppers
275ml olive oil
2 shallots, peeled and chopped
1 clove of garlic, peeled and chopped
2 tbsp pine kernels
2 tbsp grated fresh Parmesan
salt and pepper
4 large scallops

For the pasta: sift flour and salt into a bowl. Tip into food processor, add whole eggs, yolks and oil. Blend, then knead gently for 3–5 minutes. Wrap in clingfilm and set aside for 1–2 hours.

For the pesto: peel, deseed and chop peppers. Blend with oil, shallots and garlic until smooth, then remove from blender. Wash pine kernels and place in blender. Blend for 30 seconds. Add peppers, Parmesan, salt and pepper.

Prepare scallops by removing roe and 'skirt'.

Sear scallops in a hot pan with a little olive oil (for 30 seconds) and leave to cool.

Roll pasta to the thinnest gauge.

On a well-floured table, lay out the sheet of pasta and cut 8 rounds with a 6cm fluted cutter.

Place 1 scallop on top of each of 4 rounds, egg wash round and place a second round of pasta on top. Take care to seal well (with a smaller cutter or by pinching with your fingers), removing all air from the ravioli.

Poach for 3–4 minutes in water, with a little olive oil and plenty of salt. Serve with warmed red pesto.

Baked breast of farmhouse chicken

enclosing a sweet pepper mousse, accompanied by a polenta pancake and crispy spinach with a claret jus

1 breast of chicken (175g)
150g spinach
olive oil, for frying
for the sweet pepper mousse
1 red pepper
50g minced chicken breast
2 egg whites
salt and pepper
275ml double cream
for the polenta
275ml water
50g butter
75g maize flour
2 egg yolks
5g each chervil, chives and
tarragon, chopped
for the jus
100g total of carrots, onions, celery,
celeriac and leek, roughly chopped
1 glass of claret
150 ml chicken stock
100g butter

To prepare chicken breast, remove skin and bone and then flatten to 1cm escalope.
For the sweet pepper mousse: grill whole red pepper until skin blackens, then remove skin, stalk and seeds, and purée.
Chill minced chicken over ice (in an ice bain-marie). Add 2 egg whites, salt and pepper, and gradually add cream, allowing mousse to thicken. Add puréed pepper. Rest in fridge.
For the polenta: boil water with 25g butter, salt and pepper, and add maize flour. Cook until mixture thickens. Allow to cool, add 2 egg yolks and chopped herbs. Spread out on a tray to 1cm thick and allow to cool. Cut with a 6cm cutter and gently pan-fry with a 25g knob of butter.

Season a piece of tinfoil and, on it, place the breast of chicken. Spread mousse over chicken breast and roll up chicken breast in the tinfoil. Seal tinfoil parcel very quickly in a hot, dry pan and then bake in a hot oven for 10 minutes (200°C/gas mark 6). Remove chicken from oven, and from pan, and allow to rest.

For the jus: in the same pan, gently fry chopped vegetables in half the butter. Allow to colour. Add claret and reduce by half. Add chicken stock, bring to the boil and simmer for a few minutes. Sieve into a clean pan. Add remaining 50g cold, hard butter. Season.
Wash and dry spinach. Finely shred, deep-fry in hot oil, drain and season. Unwrap chicken, place polenta pancake on plate and slice chicken around. Top with spinach and surround with jus. Bon appétit!

Peter Fleming
Cameron House

Fillet of turbot

resting on braised fennel and tomato with crisp
aubergine and olive oil dressing

1 bulb of fennel
plain flour, to dust
50ml olive oil
4 plum tomatoes
1 large aubergine, finely sliced
salt
50g black olives, chopped
12 lemon segments
10g dill, chopped
10g tarragon, chopped
5g parsley
1 clove of garlic, chopped
4 x 125g turbot fillets
25g butter

To prepare fennel, cut into rings, dust with flour and pan-fry in a little olive oil for 5 minutes. Dry off with kitchen towel.

To prepare tomatoes, score tops and blanch whole in hot water for 8–10 seconds. Transfer to iced water, before removing skins. Cut tomato into petals, removing seeds.

Salt and rinse the aubergine slices, then dry thoroughly and deep-fry in a little olive oil.

To make sauce, combine 30ml olive oil, chopped olives, lemon segments, chopped herbs and garlic, and warm through.

Roast the turbot for 3 minutes each side in a hot pan with remainder of olive oil and the butter.

To serve, pile up the fennel slices and tomato petals. Place turbot on the side. Garnish with fried aubergine slices.

Peter Fleming
Cameron House

Dark chocolate tart

with white chocolate ice cream and vanilla custard

for the sweet pastry
125g butter
125g castor sugar
310g plain flour
1 egg
1 vanilla pod

for the tart
75ml double cream
150ml full cream milk
2 small eggs
185g dark chocolate, in chunks

for the ice cream
275ml full cream milk
3 yolks
40g castor sugar
100g white chocolate, in chunks

for the sauce anglaise
275ml full cream milk
1 vanilla pod
4 yolks
40g castor sugar

for the chocolate squares
30g white chocolate
30g dark chocolate

for the garnish
12 raspberries
2 stalks of redcurrants
4 sprigs of mint

For the sweet pastry: place butter and sugar in a mixing bowl and beat together until butter is pale. Slowly add flour and egg, combining until mixture holds together. Split vanilla pod lengthways and remove seeds. Add to mix. Rest for 20 minutes.
Roll out pastry to 2.5mm thick. Line 4 individual moulds, and bake blind at 200°C/gas mark 6 for 15-20 minutes.
For the tart: boil cream and milk, add eggs, and pour over chocolate.
Pour into sweet pastry moulds and cook at 150°C/gas mark 2 for 15–20 minutes.
For the ice cream: boil milk. Mix yolks and sugar until pale in colour. Pour boiled milk over yolk mix and return to stove. Cook until mixture coats the back of a spoon. Add chocolate. Let mixture cool, then churn as required.
For the sauce anglaise: boil milk with vanilla pod. Mix yolks and sugar until pale in colour. Pour boiled milk over yolk mix and return to stove. Cook until mixture coats the back of a spoon.
For the chocolate squares: in a bain-marie, melt white chocolate.
Spread evenly on to cellophane paper. With a blunt knife, score chocolate in parallel lines, 2mm apart. Place in fridge for 5 minutes to set.
In a bain-marie, melt dark chocolate. Spread on to set white chocolate. Allow to set in fridge and cut into squares.
Serve as shown.

Neil Forbes
Atrium

I believe that taste is everything in cooking. Not enough restaurants are focusing on taste these days; instead they're concentrating on the prettiness of the dish, on making the food look good rather than drawing on the quality of the raw ingredients. For example, one of the dishes I've chosen to do – turbot fillet roasted on garden thyme with an endive tart tatin – is very simple, but the combination of complex flavours is unbeatable!

As a chef, I've been heavily influenced by the French, in particular three great chefs: Joel Robouchon, Alain Ducasse and the late Fernand Point of La Pyramide. I read a lot and have far too many cookery books for my own good, but they do provide a great source of inspiration – we are always trying to extend our repertoire at the Atrium.

I'm a firm believer in seasonality and get depressed when I see strawberries on the menu in January. Let's use local produce at the right time! I also find it very depressing that there are so many themed and chain restaurants now, taking away business from the real professionals. When I worked at Braeval, which was in the middle of nowhere, people used to come from Glasgow, Stirling, Edinburgh. They made the effort and I think they thought it was worth it. People need to support local, independent restaurants – after all, you can spend the same amount of money for a meal in a chain restaurant as you can in a place like the Atrium, but the quality of the food, the cooking and the overall experience are so much better here.

I suppose I don't think you should be a chef if you're in it for the money – if I wanted to make serious money, I'd be a lawyer or accountant. I do this job because I enjoy it, because I love working with the fantastic produce we have in Scotland. I love the fact that my job is about working as part of a team and about teaching. I see my role as supporting my staff and working with them to do the best.

Pomme ratte

with fillings of egg, caviar, pink peppercorn butter,
spring onion crème fraîche and smoked salmon

20 thumb-sized potatoes
salt
2 tbsp olive oil
1 tsp pink peppercorns
50g unsalted butter, softened
1 large shallot, finely diced
1 tsp chives, finely chopped
1 spring onion, finely chopped
4 tsp crème fraîche
2 large, free range eggs, hard-boiled
1 tsp chopped flat-leaf parsley
4 large handfuls of rock salt
50g smoked salmon, cut into thin strips
4 tsp Keta caviar
4 tsp Sevruga caviar
4 small sprigs of chervil

Wash potatoes, dry and sprinkle with a little salt. Cut lengthways about $^1/_3$ cm depth into potatoes. Roast in oil in a moderate oven (180°C/gas mark 4) for 15–20 minutes until tender, then keep in a warm place.

To make the butter, add pink peppercorns to the softened butter with a little of the chopped shallot and all the chopped chives. Shape butter into barrel shapes and refrigerate.

Add spring onion to crème fraîche, season and set aside. Shell hard-boiled eggs and, separating the white from the yellow, grate on the fine side of a grater. Then, in a small bowl, combine chopped flat-leaf parsley with remaining shallot.

You are now ready to 'plate up'. Place a large handful of rock salt on to 4 flat plates. Slightly squeeze potatoes like baked potatoes. Fill 1 with the crème fraîche, 1 with the butter, 1 with the smoked salmon and 1 with both caviars. The remaining potato fill with half a teaspoon of egg white and egg yolk, and top with the shallot and parsley mix. Arrange attractively on to the rock salt and garnish with chervil. Repeat three times and serve immediately.

Turbot fillet

roasted on garden thyme, endive tart tatin

4 large Belgium endive
200g unsalted butter
100g castor sugar
4 x 15cm (diameter) discs of
rolled-out puff pastry (good bought
pastry is okay)
4 x 150g turbot fillets cut into
squares, boned and skinned (get
your fishmonger to do this)
Maldon sea salt
freshly ground pepper
200g freshest possible garden-
picked thyme
juice of 1 lemon
You will need 4 small black cast-
iron blini pans

In a thick-bottomed pan boil endive for 7–10 minutes until just tender or until a knife can be inserted easily. Refresh in cold water.

In a small blini pan, melt 25g of butter and 25g of sugar. Bring to a light caramel stage. Meanwhile cut whole endive in half lengthways and place both parts into caramel. Caramelise for 4–5 minutes on a low heat. Allow to cool and cover with puff pastry disc. Repeat with other endives. Place in a moderate oven (180°C/gas mark 4) and cook pastry until golden brown (approximately 10 minutes), remove from oven and allow to rest. To cook turbot, place a frying pan on to a high heat. Place remaining butter into the pan, take it to a frothing temperature and add turbot fillets. Season with Maldon salt and pepper and place into a roasting tray with garden thyme. Roast in oven (200°C/gas mark 6, for 4–5 minutes) until golden brown, but still moist. Check this by touching with your fingers – if it gives a little, then it's perfectly cooked. Warm plates and serve turbot on the roasted thyme. On separate plates turn out endive tart tatins, season with salt and pepper. Squeeze lemon juice on to fish and serve immediately.

Loin of Perthshire lamb

with lamb pithivier, barley and root vegetable jus

for the lamb pithivier

150g unsalted butter
1/2 tsp garlic, finely chopped
50g shallot, finely diced
200g small dice of lamb rump
1 tbsp wild mushrooms, chopped
1 tsp tarragon, chopped
1/2 tsp Périgord truffle, finely chopped
salt and freshly ground pepper
100g small dice of carrot, cooked
100g small dice of turnip, cooked
100g small dice of celeriac, cooked
8 x 7cm (diameter) discs of ready-rolled puff pastry (again good quality bought pastry is okay)
1 egg yolk (for egg wash)
2 tbsp olive oil
4 x 175g well-trimmed loins of lamb (get your butcher to trim off any sinew or connective tissue from the lamb loins)
4 handfuls of large leaf spinach, stems removed and washed

for the root vegetable and barley jus

100ml white wine
100g barley (soaked for 1 hour)
1 litre good lamb stock
1 sprig of rosemary

For the lamb pithivier: heat a little of the butter in a thick-bottomed pan and sweat garlic and shallots until translucent, then add dice of lamb rump. Cook until golden brown and add mushrooms. Continue to cook for a further 2 minutes and add tarragon and truffle. Season and allow to cool, then add half of the carrot, turnip and celeriac.

Take 4 puff pastry discs and place 1 tablespoon of lamb mixture into centre of each disc. Place other 4 pastry discs over the mixture and pinch the edges so that none of the mixture will escape while cooking. Make an attractive swirl effect on each pithivier and egg wash. Bake in a moderate oven (180°C/gas mark 4) for 8–10 minutes until golden brown.

While the pithiviers are cooking, place a large black cast-iron frying pan on to a high heat. Add 1 tablespoon of oil. Season loins of lamb with salt and pepper and place into hot oil, allow to colour slightly and add the remaining butter. Season and cook to the required degree, i.e. medium rare. Allow to rest. Remove pithiviers from the oven and rest. In a thick-bottomed pan, heat another tablespoon of olive oil and throw in washed and picked spinach. Season. Cook for 1 minute and drain.

To 'plate up' place a tablespoon of spinach on each plate. Place the pithivier on to the spinach and with a sharp knife slice lamb loin into 6 pieces or so and make a crescent shape at the bottom of the plate. Serve immediately with root vegetable and barley jus.

For the root vegetable and barley jus: in a thick-bottomed pan reduce white wine by two-thirds. Meanwhile, cook soaked barley until just tender. Add lamb stock to white wine reduction and reduce at a fast boil until desired consistency is reached. At the last minute, add sprig of rosemary and infuse for 2 minutes. The barley and remaining diced, cooked carrot, turnip and celeriac can now be added. Season and serve immediately.

Caramelised rice pudding
with apricots and toasted almonds

150g pudding rice
1 tbsp butter
500ml coconut milk
500ml full fat milk
150g castor sugar
1 vanilla pod, split
80g cooked apricots
30g sultanas
30g toasted almonds
good dusting of icing sugar
for the garnish
100ml water
50g castor sugar
1 vanilla pod

Wash and rinse rice well and, in a thick-bottomed pan, melt butter. Add rice, milk, sugar and vanilla pod. Bring to the boil and simmer for 30–40 minutes until thick and gloopy. Dice 30g of the apricots and add to the rice with the sultanas.

Line a ramekin with clingfilm and fill with rice. Allow to set for 10 minutes or so. Turn out into a warm bowl, garnish with toasted almond and apricots. Dust with icing sugar and caramelise with a blowtorch.

Make stock syrup with water and sugar. Bring to the boil and reduce for 1 minute. Cut vanilla pod into very thin strips. Cut the remaining 50g of apricots into batons. Cook in stock syrup for 2–3 minutes.

Serve immediately, drizzling syrup liberally around.

Jimmy and Amanda Graham
Ostlers Close

Jimmy: Up to the age of six, my parents ran a hotel in Kingussie and I loved helping my mum in the kitchen. I wanted to be a baker, but there were no positions, so I started as a chef in a hotel in Pitlochry. The biggest influence on me as a chef was Sammi Denzler – he was a lecturer at Napier where I studied Catering Craft and I worked for him at Denzler's in Hanover Street during and after college.

Amanda: I met Jimmy when I took a summer job in a restaurant in St. Andrews. I was studying medicine at Glasgow at the time. I went back to university for a year, but then gave up and went into business with Jimmy, running this restaurant. Jimmy does most of the cooking and I work front of house, but I help with all the preparations. The first ten years were very hard work, but it's great now (after nearly twenty years) because we have a loyal clientele who come all year round.

Jimmy: We've always used only local produce – everything must be fresh and in season. A local rare-breeder supplies us with Jacob Sheep – the lamb in November tastes like new season lamb. We have good sources for free range duck, hand-dived scallops and all the organic vegetables and herbs we require. I love wild mushrooms and spend the autumn hunting them in Perthshire. I like to experiment in my cooking, so our food is always developing and changing.

Amanda: It's hard work running a restaurant. We never really stop – even on our days off, there is always something to do. We love doing our own thing, running this place the way we want to. I've never regretted giving up medicine and, in a way, I use a lot of my knowledge and skills in this job – a lot of working front of house is about attention to detail and observation. We have two daughters and we'd like to spend more time with them, but we are lucky that they go to local schools and that my parents can help out looking after them.

Jimmy and Amanda Graham
Ostlers Close

Seared Isle of Mull scallops
with a rösti style fishcake

120g chopped, mixed fish, e.g. salmon, monkfish, cod

20g chopped mixed herbs, e.g. flat-leaf parsley, chive, chervil, basil

1 clove of garlic, crushed

60g onion, finely diced

20g Dijon mustard

500g Maris Piper or similar waxy potato

2 egg yolks

1 tsp fresh chilli, finely diced

20g freshly grated Parmesan

olive oil

12 large hand-dived scallops

for the basil oil

100g olive oil

30g basil

salt and pepper

for the herb mayonnaise

3 tbsp mayonnaise

30g chopped herbs (chervil, flat-leaf parsley, chives or basil)

2 spring onions, finely chopped

Marinade the chopped, mixed fish with the herbs, garlic, onion and mustard for at least 1 hour before. Place in the fridge.

Oil 4 metal rings (8cm diameter, 5cm depth) with olive oil.

Peel potatoes, roughly grate into a clean tea towel and squeeze firmly to take out excess liquid. Place potato in a large bowl, add fish mix, egg yolks, chilli and Parmesan. Mix well.

Put oiled rings into a large flat frying pan, with enough oil to coat the base. Allow to heat until hot, fill rings evenly with rösti mix. Press down with spoon to pack ring. Cook until browned on one side. Turn over, then place whole pan in oven for roughly 5 minutes to cook through.

Put another pan on heat with oil, allow to smoke before sealing scallops on one side until caramelised. Flip over and remove from heat.

Place rösti cake on hot plates in centre, arrange scallops round.

Rösti can be topped with a small amount of herb mayonnaise and scallops served with basil oil.

Pan-fried terrine of potato and duck leg confit

with chanterelles

for the duck leg confit

(to be made at least one day in advance)

3 duck legs

salt

100g duck fat (or lard)

for the marinade

1 tbsp soy sauce

1 tbsp balsamic vinegar

1 dessertspoon sesame oil

1 dessertspoon maple syrup

1 dessertspoon chilli sauce

for the terrine

2 kg Maris Piper or similar waxy potatoes

3/4 litre olive oil for cooking

duck leg confit (see above)

40g fresh coriander, chopped

4 spring onions, finely chopped

500ml duck stock

1 tbsp plum sauce

100ml red wine

150g chanterelles

For the duck leg confit: rub the duck legs in a layer of salt and refrigerate for 1 day. Wash off salt and pat them dry. Melt fat in roasting tin and poach duck legs until soft in a very slow oven (e.g. overnight at 80°C or the lowest oven setting).

Allow fat and cooking juices to settle and skim fat from the top. Use cooking juices for stock. Cover duck legs with the fat and store in fridge (sealed), when cold.

Peel potatoes, cut off sides to square up potatoes before slicing on a mandolin (this allows them to sit better in the terrine). Fry potatoes in oil in batches and set aside in a separate roasting tin.

Remove duck from bone and shred, put in a bowl with the marinade, along with coriander and spring onions.

Oil then line a 28cm terrine with clingfilm. Layer round base and sides with sliced potatoes 3 layers thick. Press firmly into position then put in a layer of duck followed by another layer of potatoes, 3 deep again. Repeat until finishing with a layer of potatoes on top.

Fold over clingfilm. Cut a piece of hard card the same size as the top of the terrine. Cover with foil then clingfilm. Place on top of terrine and put on weights to press. Place in fridge for a minimum of 24 hours.

Reduce duck stock until it's dark, add plum sauce and red wine and reduce again until sticky.

Slice terrine into 3cm portions, put in a hot pan with a little oil, sear on one side until brown, then place on a baking tray to finish cooking in a moderate oven (190°C/gas mark 5) for 5 minutes. Fry chanterelles in olive oil until just cooked.

To serve, place terrine browned side up with chanterelles round the outside and trickle the sauce sparingly around mushrooms.

Jimmy and Amanda Graham
Ostlers Close

Pig's trotter
stuffed with oxtail on potato mash

2 hind pig's trotters, cooked
3 whole oxtail, cooked
1kg potatoes
200ml milk
60g butter
500ml cooking juices from oxtail
braising
250ml red wine
1 tbsp redcurrant jelly
(Serves 6–8)

Remove meat from pig's trotters and shred. Mix a little of the fat and the cooking jelly with the meat.

Roll out a long piece of foil (roughly 25cm in length) and place meat down the centre. Roll foil tightly around meat to make a sausage shape, twist ends and place in fridge overnight.

Remove all oxtail meat from bones. Open out foil from pork and press oxtail meat round the centre core of pork meat. Re-roll into a sausage shape and again refrigerate overnight.

Boil potatoes in salted water until soft. Drain and dry over a gentle heat. Put milk and butter into a pan and bring to the boil. When butter is fully melted, pour over potatoes and mash.

To make sauce, strain 500ml of cooking juices from the oxtail into a pan. Bring to the boil, reduce by half, add red wine and redcurrant jelly then reduce by half again.

Unwrap oxtail, cut into thick slices and heat through in a moderate oven for 10 minutes.

Place on top of potato mash and drizzle sauce around the plate.

Steamed tayberry and syrup sponge
on a cream custard

125g castor sugar
125g Flora (best result as opposed to butter)
2 large eggs
125g self-raising flour
1 tsp baking powder
200ml stock syrup, (made from 200g granulated white sugar and 200ml water)
300g tayberries
2 tbsp golden syrup
a dash of crème de framboise (optional)
for the custard
100ml semi-skimmed milk
250ml double cream
1 vanilla pod, split
3 egg yolks
100g castor sugar
for the raspberry coulis
125g raspberries
100ml water
30g castor sugar

(Serves 6)

The key to a good steamed sponge is to use individual 200ml plastic basins with snap-on lids, and a pan for steaming with a tight-fitting lid.

Cream sugar and Flora, adding eggs one at a time with addition of 1 tablespoon of flour with each egg. Add remaining flour and baking powder. Beat well, till light and creamy. Set aside.

Bring stock syrup to the boil, add tayberries and simmer for 1 minute. Remove fruit from liquid, dividing between pudding basins. Return liquid to the heat, boil and reduce to a third, then add golden syrup and framboise, stir, and spoon 1 tablespoon into each basin.

Divide sponge mix between basins and snap on the lids.

Put enough water in the pan to reach halfway up pudding basins, bring to the boil, place basins in pan, put on lid and steam for roughly 3/4 hour. The basins will bounce to touch when ready. Don't boil water too hard otherwise it will boil dry.

For the custard: put milk and cream on to boil with the vanilla pod. As it reaches the boil remove it from heat and scrape seeds from pod into milk/cream mix. Beat egg yolks and sugar in a mixing bowl until thick and creamy yellow. Bring cream mix back to the boil and pour into egg mixture. Blend well and return to a gentle heat, stirring regularly till thickened – do not boil.

The custard sauce can be feathered with a little raspberry coulis and sponge topped with ice cream.

For the raspberry coulis: mix all ingredients in a pan, bring to the boil, simmer for a couple of minutes then blend and sieve.

Simon Haigh and Matthew Gray
Inverlochy Castle

Simon: Inverlochy was built in 1863 by the first Lord Abinger and was a family home for over a century, until it was converted to a country house hotel in 1969. Since then, there have only been five chefs. The first chef was a woman called Mary Shaw who was the private cook of the Hobbs family (who bought the castle in 1946); Mary played a key role in establishing Inverlochy's reputation for fine dining and, in 1974, she was awarded the MBE for 'services to cooking'.

Matthew: Simon has recently left Inverlochy after eight years and I have taken over as Chef de Cuisine, having been sous chef here for the last five years.

Our approach to food is to use produce in season. The menu is dictated by what's fresh and what's good – Scottish seafood and game are a regular and popular feature of the menu. Obviously, we're not a city restaurant, but we do need to keep up with food fashions to a certain extent – we have lots of travelling guests who have expectations of 'the latest' as well as 'the best' food. So we follow fashion, but are not dictated by it – we are not going to use white truffle oil just because it's new! Our main aim is to maintain a quality and individuality in all our dishes. We focus on cooking food that goes naturally together, that marries well.

The best compliment you can have is repeat guests – we have some guests who come back every year, and have been doing so for fifteen to twenty years. They are looking for continuity and we can offer that. The staff we have in the kitchen tend to stay a long time. We train up people, giving them experience in every part of the kitchen; that's what happened with me – I came from Knockinaam Lodge in Portpatrick. It certainly helps that Michael Leonard, Inverlochy Castle's managing director, has been in charge since 1976.

Puff pastry pillow of asparagus

topped with pan-fried foie gras

for the Madeira sauce

4 shallots, finely chopped
10g butter
1 head of garlic, cut in half, horizontally
1 sprig of thyme
1.5kg mushrooms, sliced
2 tbsp sherry vinegar
1 bottle of Madeira
1 litre chicken stock
200ml veal glace
200g morels, dried
4 puff pastry cases
4 button mushrooms, sliced
salt and pepper
100ml double cream
20 asparagus spears
4 x 75g slices finest quality foie gras (duck or goose)
sherry vinegar
4 sprigs of chervil

For the Madeira sauce: sweat shallots and garlic in butter with sprig of thyme. Add mushrooms and cook in oven (190°C/gas mark 5) for 20 minutes, until dry. Deglaze with sherry vinegar. Add Madeira, reduce by half. Add chicken stock and veal glace. Reduce to required thickness and add reconstituted dried morels.

For the puff pastry cases, good-quality frozen pastry will do fine. Cut into rectangles, cook at 200°C/gas mark 6 for 12-16 minutes and hollow out (retaining lids).

Quickly sauté button mushrooms, season with salt and pepper. Add cream and reduce to coating consistency. Keep warm.

Cook asparagus in a steamer for 4–6 minutes and refresh in iced water. Reheat when ready to serve in emulsion of salted water and butter.

In a very hot pan, sear foie gras for 2 minutes on one side. Turn over and season. Cook for 1 minute on other side. Pour off excess fat, deglaze with sherry vinegar, place on kitchen paper and reserve.

To serve, place pillow in centre of plate and spoon in mushroom mixture. Put 5 spears of asparagus on the top. Place foie gras on top of that. Pour Madeira sauce over the top, replace the lid and add a sprig of chervil.

Mallaig turbot

with roasted Scottish lobster

200g shallots, sliced
110g unsalted butter
200g mushrooms, sliced
500ml Noilly Prat
2 lobster (approximately 700g in weight)
4 x 225g turbot steaks
1 tbsp melted butter
salt and pepper
3 tbsp double cream
1 bunch of chives
2 tomatoes, deseeded and chopped
1/2 tbsp vegetable oil
juice of 1/2 lemon

To make braising liquor, sweat shallots in 10g butter and add mushrooms. When cooked, add Noilly Prat. Reduce by half and reserve.
Cut lobster through shell into chunks (known as collops). Cook claws for 4 minutes in boiling salted water, refresh in cold water, then release from shell and reserve.
Put 2 tablespoons of braising liquor in a pan, place turbot on top, then brush with melted butter and season with salt and pepper.
Bring to the boil on top of stove and place in a moderate oven (190°C/gas mark 5) for 3 minutes with lid on.
Remove and strain liquor from pan. Keep turbot in a warm place.
Add cream to braising liquor and gradually whisk in remaining butter until fully incorporated, then add the chopped chives and tomatoes at the last minute.
Heat a non-stick pan, add a little oil (enough to coat the pan) and sear collops – 2 minutes each side. In the final minute, add claws, season with salt and pepper and a couple of drops of lemon juice.
Place turbot in the centre of the plate, arrange claw meat on top and the collops around the claw meat. Pour sauce over and then serve with vegetables (we suggest asparagus, baby leeks, spinach and roasted fennel).

Simon Haigh and Matthew Gray
Inverlochy Castle

Beef and mushrooms

with herb crust

for the Madeira sauce

4 shallots, finely chopped
10g butter
1 head of garlic, cut in half, horizontally
1 sprig of thyme
1.5kg mushrooms, sliced
2 tbsp sherry vinegar
1 bottle of Madeira
1 litre chicken stock
200ml veal glace

12 whole shallots
water
50g butter
pinch of sugar
salt and pepper
100g dried bread (white, crusts removed)
40g parsley, curly or flat-leaf, stalks removed
1 clove of garlic
10ml olive oil
1kg celeriac
275ml skimmed milk
1 clove of garlic
1 sprig of thyme
4 x 175g fillet steaks
500g mushrooms, diced
50g butter
2 tbsp grain mustard
12 new potatoes (roseval), boiled
12 celery leaves, deep-fried

For the Madeira sauce: sweat shallots and garlic in butter with sprig of thyme. Add mushrooms and cook in oven (190°C/gas mark 5) for 20 minutes, until dry. Deglaze with sherry vinegar. Add Madeira, reduce by half. Add chicken stock and veal glace. Reduce to required thickness.

Put shallots, butter, sugar and salt and pepper in a pan and half-cover with water, boil and reduce down until all water evaporates and shallots start to caramelise (approximately 15–20 minutes).

Blitz bread, parsley, garlic and salt and pepper in a processor. When mixture is bright green, add olive oil while still mixing.

Cook celeriac in skimmed milk with garlic and thyme until soft. Purée and sieve.

Sear fillets in hot pan until well coloured and sealed. Cook to just under preferred state (rare, medium etc), to allow for reheating.

Cook diced mushrooms in butter.

Brush top of each fillet with grain mustard, and divide out mushroom mix between each steak. Liberally coat with herb breadcrumbs.

Place steak in oven to reheat, arrange celeriac purée, new potatoes and shallots around plate as desired.

Remove steaks from oven and colour a little under grill.

Place in centre of plate, pour Madeira sauce around, add deep-fried celery leaves on top of the purée and serve.

Roast peaches

with a warm raspberry coulis

570ml stock syrup (made from
570ml water and 500g sugar)
1 split vanilla pod
4 peaches, firm but ripe
50g butter
25g sugar
24 raspberries, to garnish
4 sprigs of mint, to garnish

for the nougatine
4 eggs
80g castor sugar
20g honey
seeds of 1 vanilla pod
150g candied fruit
45g roasted, flaked almonds
45g roasted hazelnuts
45g pistachio nuts
500ml double cream

for the macaroons
225g icing sugar
125g ground almonds
120g egg white
25g castor sugar

for the coulis
250g raspberries
100ml stock syrup (made from
100ml water and 100g sugar)
juice of $\frac{1}{2}$ lemon

for the brandy snap discs
50g butter
50g castor sugar
50g glucose
50g soft flour

First of all make stock syrup by adding sugar to water and bringing to the boil; remove from heat and strain.

Bring stock syrup and vanilla pod to boil. Add halved peaches, and simmer for 5–10 minutes or until starting to soften. Remove from heat and leave to cool in cooking liquid. Peel and reserve.

For the nougatine: line a terrine with greaseproof paper. Whisk eggs, sugar, honey and vanilla seeds to ribbon stage. Whisk mixture over a bain-marie until light and fluffy, then leave to cool. Fold in fruit and nuts. Whisk cream until soft peak stage and fold into mixture. Place in terrine and freeze. When frozen, cut into 1cm discs.

For the macaroons: preheat oven to 190°C/gas mark 5. Line a baking sheet with greaseproof paper. Sieve icing sugar and ground almonds together. Whisk egg whites until they form soft peaks, slowly add castor sugar and whisk until firm peak stage. Fold in icing sugar and ground almonds until smooth. Put mixture into a piping bag fitted with a plain 5mm nozzle then pipe macaroons to the required size on to the baking sheet. Leave to rest for 10–15 minutes to allow surface to become dry then bake for 10–12 minutes, leaving oven door ajar (to let steam out).

For the coulis: put all ingredients in a pan, bring to the boil, liquidise and sieve.

For the brandy snap discs: combine ingredients to form a paste and leave to rest. Place small blobs of mixture on tray and bake in hot oven (200°C/gas mark 6) for approximately 10 minutes, until golden brown. Keep in airtight container until required.

Put peaches in a hot pan with butter and sugar. Caramelise slightly. Place peaches in hot oven (200°C/ gas mark 6) for approximately 5 minutes. Warm raspberry coulis.

To serve, place a nougatine disc in centre of plate, then place a brandy snap disc on top. When peaches are ready, place one on top of brandy snap disc. Pour raspberry coulis around. Sprinkle with crushed macaroons and garnish with 6 fresh raspberries and sprig of mint.

Andrew Hamer
Gleneagles

Food was important at home; my dad, who travelled the world as a musician, would bring back unusual and exotic ingredients. As a result, I developed an interest in food, although it was my older sister's influence that made me decide to become a chef. She worked in a hotel in Wales and I would help out there during my holidays. Discovering something I enjoyed and was good at, I went on to train as a chef at Westminster College.

After beginning my career in Langan's in London, I moved on to a hotel in Guernsey where I met my wife, who is Scottish. My first head chef post was at Ladyburn, a small country house hotel in Ayrshire, then on to work for Bill Costley at Highgrove and Lochgreen. Bill proved to be my mentor, not so much on cooking style, but in terms of the commercial side of the industry. Learning from him about managing a busy operation has proved invaluable in my work at Gleneagles.

I've worked at Gleneagles for four years and was appointed Head Chef in January 2000. It's a very hands-on job and I'm involved in the style of food and in menu development, as well as managing a brigade of forty chefs in the kitchens. Alan Hill, our Food and Beverage Manager, who was previously Executive Chef, has given me huge support.

At the moment cooking at Gleneagles is going through a cultural change – we're moving towards more seasonalised menus using the best of local produce, although I'm also very interested in looking further afield for top quality products. For instance, after I recently visited Italy on a tasting tour, we are now using a 25 year old Italian balsamic vinegar.

At Gleneagles, our approach is essentially to use the highest quality products and to keep the food simple. Our aim is to always exceed the expectations of our guests – a challenging ambition as expectations of the Gleneagles experience are very high indeed!

Andrew Hamer
Gleneagles

Warm Scottish lobster

with goose liver and smoked tomato

4 lobsters
4 vine tomatoes
30g leek, cut into lozenges
280g goose liver (70g slice per portion)
fresh chervil, to garnish

for the ravioli

8 hand-dived Oban scallops
10ml double cream
pinch of grated lemon zest
2g chives, chopped
salt and pepper
65g egg pasta

for the sauce

5g shallots
5g butter
smoked tomato trimmings
5ml cognac
60ml lobster stock
5ml double cream

Place live lobsters into boiling salted water and cook until slightly pink. Refresh in iced water. You want the lobster to be undercooked as you are going to warm it through in the sauce at a later stage.

Crack claws and remove meat from shell, cut lobsters in half and remove tail meat and place aside.

For the ravioli: blitz scallops in blender, remove and pass through sieve over a bowl of ice. Mix in double cream, lemon zest and chopped chives to form a mousse and season to taste.

Roll out pasta, place a spoonful of scallop mousse on to pasta, then place a piece of lobster claw on top and another piece of pasta on top of that.

Form a pouch by crimping the edges together and cook in simmering water with salt and a little olive oil for approximately 5–6 minutes. When cooked, place aside.

Blanch tomato, remove skin and seeds. Pat dry on paper towel. Place into a cold smoker and cold smoke for approximately 10 minutes.

Trim up tomato and finely dice.

For the sauce: sweat off shallot with butter and add smoked tomato trimmings and cognac.

Next, add lobster stock and reduce a little, add cream, adjust seasoning and pass through chinoise.

To finish, sweat off leek lozenges in a little butter and drain. Place into the middle of a soup plate and place warm ravioli on top of leek.

Warm lobster in sauce for 3 minutes, remove from sauce and place lobster around ravioli. Scatter smoked tomato around dish. Sear goose liver in a hot, dry pan and then place on top of ravioli.

Whizz up sauce with a hand blender to form a light frothy sauce. Pour sauce over lobster and garnish with fresh chervil.

Andrew Hamer
Gleneagles

Roasted veal fillet

with caramelised root vegetables and melted onions

500g Maris Piper potatoes
salt and pepper
120g carrot
120g turnip
80g leek
120g celeriac
50g butter
140ml chicken stock
400g white onions, peeled and sliced
275ml Barsac white wine
750g veal fillets
1 tbsp olive oil
40g Dijon mustard
18g tarragon, chopped
8g thyme, chopped
8g flat-leaf parsley, chopped
30g shallots
25g butter
25g thyme
1 clove of garlic
40ml Madeira
20ml 25-year-old balsamic vinegar
300ml veal stock
4 sprigs of thyme

Peel potatoes and cut into cylinders, then slice thinly.

Place into a hot rösti pan, overlapping, and season with herbs all the way up to the top of the pan and then place in the oven to cook (200°C/gas mark 6) for about 20 minutes, until crisp and golden brown. Keep warm.

Peel and cut root vegetables into triangles across the grain, and place in a hot pan with a little butter and caramelise.

Next, pour in chicken stock and finish in oven (200°C/gas mark 6) for 10 minutes until tender. Keep warm.

Sweat off onions in pan with some Barsac white wine, place lid on pan and braise slowly for 2 hours, checking frequently. When mixture is ready it should be soft and tender. Place aside and keep warm.

Trim any sinews off veal fillet, seal in a hot pan with olive oil and then roll in Dijon mustard and chopped mixed fresh herbs.

Roast through in oven on a vegetable trivet until cooked pink (200°C/gas mark 6) for 8-10 minutes.

Sweat off shallots in butter, add thyme, garlic, Madeira and aged balsamic vinegar and reduce.

Next, add veal stock and reduce again. Pass through fine sieve and adjust seasoning.

To serve, place potato cake in the middle of the plate and stack up rustic vegetables on top.

Place 3 teaspoonfuls of melted white onion around the plate, then cut veal and place on top of white onions. Finally, pour sauce around and finish with sprig of thyme on top of vegetable stack.

Andrew Hamer
Gleneagles

Seared wild sea bass

with marinated anchovies and shellfish gravy

for the aubergine caviar

1 baking potato
450g aubergine
15g garlic
1 sprig of thyme
2 bay leaves
salt and pepper
100ml olive oil

for the shellfish gravy

28g shallots, finely chopped
25g butter
1 piece of star anise
30ml brandy
500ml langoustine stock
30ml double cream

for the garnish

80g vine tomatoes
35g white anchovies
20g pine kernels

480g wild sea bass (skin left on)
28g sea salt
4 sprigs of basil

for the basil oil

50g basil
50g parsley
60ml olive oil

For the aubergine caviar: place potato in the oven and bake until soft. Cut aubergine in half, score with a knife and rub flesh with garlic. Drizzle with olive oil and sprinkle with thyme leaves and bay leaves, then season. Roast in a hot oven (180°C/gas mark 4) for approximately 20 minutes until soft, then remove the bay and thyme leaves and scrape out the flesh. Blitz in processor with olive oil and half the baked potato (the other half of the potato is not used), season to taste then pass through a fine sieve and keep warm.

For the shellfish gravy: sweat off finely chopped shallots in butter, then add the star anise, brandy and reduce with langoustine stock. Once the stock has reduced by three-quarters, add double cream and reduce for a minute, then season to taste and pass through fine chinoise. Keep warm.

For the garnish: take tomatoes, remove eye and score top. Blanch and remove skin and quarter, then remove seeds and pat dry. Square off the tomato petals and then dice into even squares. Cut anchovy fillets into the same size of dice. Roast pine kernels in oven for a few minutes until golden brown. Place on a plate in alternate circles. Set aside.

Fillet and scale sea bass. Score sea bass 3 times on the skin side and then season with sea salt and milled pepper.

For the basil oil: add basil and parsley to olive oil, blitz and pass through a fine chinoise.

To finish, place a little olive oil and a knob of butter in a hot pan. Place sea bass skin side down and cook until skin is crispy. When you see the flesh of the fish start to go white, flip over and finish for a few seconds on the flesh side.
Place the plate in the oven or under a grill to warm it up, then place aubergine caviar in the middle.
Next, place sea bass on top, then whizz gravy up into a foam and spoon around the garnish with a sprig of basil.
Drizzle with basil oil.

141

Baked lemon curd

for the lemon curd
200g butter
100g crème fraîche
2 eggs
1 egg yolk
juice of 3-4 lemons
140g sugar
2 leaves of gelatine

for the pastry
75g icing sugar
1 egg
1 egg yolk
pinch of salt
grated zest of $\frac{1}{2}$ lemon
250g soft flour or plain flour
125g soft butter
125g dark chocolate

for the tuille
200g icing sugar
200g soft flour, mixed well
4 egg whites

for the sugar spirals
250g water
500g sugar
100g glucose
lemon juice

for the raspberry compote
200g raspberries
100g castor sugar
 juice of $\frac{1}{2}$ lemon
icing sugar, to garnish
assorted fruits, to garnish

Melt butter in bain-marie and add the other lemon curd ingredients, except for the gelatine. Cook out, then add gelatine and remove from the heat. Mix well and sieve. Allow to cool slightly.

Mix egg yolk, egg and sugar together. Add pinch salt and lemon zest. Rub butter into flour and mix together. Allow to rest in fridge before using. Roll out pastry, cut out and place into 6cm ring and bake for about 12 minutes (180°C/gas mark 4). Remove from oven and allow to cool in the ring.

Pour in lemon mixture and allow to chill. Once chilled, melt dark chocolate and spread on to acetate; remove ring and bend chocolate around lemon curd.

For the tuille: spread mix on to template and bake in oven to colour for 2-3 minutes (150°C/gas mark 2). Hold base of tuille and pull up top to form a spiral.

For the sugar spirals: dissolve water and sugar. Add glucose and bring to the boil. Cook to 175°C, brushing down where necessary. Remove from heat and add a couple of drops of lemon juice to stop any crystallisation. Dip spoon in and spiral around steel.

For the raspberry compote: mix together and cook for approximately 5 minutes to form compote.

To serve, place tuille on to middle of plate and put lemon curd on top. Place sugar spiral in middle and place raspberry compote around quenelle of crème fraîche on top of curd. Dust with icing sugar. Place assorted fruits on plate for decoration.

Tony Heath
Let's Eat

I come from Dorset and trained in hotel management. I became General Manager of a variety of hotels up and down the country, including one in Edinburgh – that was my first experience of Scotland and I loved it. After a time back in England, I got a job at Huntingtower in Perth and, when the chef left, I decided to try my hand in the kitchen – I'd always enjoyed cooking, so I took on the job. I loved it, but it was hard work being chef and manager at the same time! In the 1980s, I opened the Coach House, here in Perth. The place was a success, but I did think that there must be easier ways of making money! After all these years, I'm not so sure!

For a while, I ran my own wine shop in St. Andrews – the nicest wine shop you've ever seen – but not a success. I realised I needed to be more 'hands on' and busy. I went back into management and worked at Murrayshall, where Bruce Sangster was the chef and where I met my partner Shona Drysdale.

I always knew I wanted to be my own boss. I've always believed in giving my all to whatever I do and, anyway, I was itching to get back into the kitchen. To cut a long story short, Shona and I set up a restaurant in Aberdeen – well, in the end, two restaurants (the Courtyard I and II).

We came back to Perth and opened Let's Eat in 1995. It was very daunting at first because the premises were bigger than any we'd had before, but luckily there were loyal customers almost waiting for our return. There had been no new restaurants in Perth for years, so we were busy from day one. The style here is informal – we want customers to feel relaxed and to have the kind of meal they want. Food is prepared simply, from the best local and seasonal produce available. Our ambitions are to keep going, keep making our regulars happy and keep them coming back for more!

Gratin of dived Skye scallops and artichoke

with crispy leeks

1kg Jerusalem artichokes, washed, peeled and sliced thinly (use a mandolin for evenness)
1 medium potato, peeled, washed and sliced as above
1 tsp salt and ground black pepper
600ml double cream
1 clove of garlic, finely chopped
pinch of nutmeg
100g Gruyère cheese, grated
vegetable oil for deep frying
2 medium leeks, washed, cut into thin strips
8–12 scallops (allow 2–3 per person depending on size)
olive oil for sautéing

Lay out sliced artichoke and potato on a tray. Sprinkle over salt and leave for 10 minutes. Heat cream with garlic and nutmeg and pepper. Squeeze out as much of the liquid from the now soft artichokes and potatoes with your hands and place them in hot cream, stirring well over the heat, allowing them to amalgamate. Pour mixture into an ovenproof dish, arrange and press down so that you have an even covering of the dish; try and have a depth of about 4cm. Sprinkle over Gruyère and place dish in a moderate oven (190°C/gas mark 5) for about 40 minutes, until cooked.

Heat oil in deep pan to 170°C. Fry leeks until crispy and lift out on to kitchen paper. Salt very lightly.

Remove roes from scallops. Heat a non-stick frying pan, brush scallops with olive oil and season lightly. Sauté in pan for 1 minute either side. They should be lightly caramelised and soft in the middle. Remove and keep warm.

Using a round cutter, cut out roundels of gratin and place on to hot plates. Arrange scallops around and on top of gratin. Drizzle some extra virgin olive oil around and lightly place a pile of crispy leeks on top.

Coriander-crusted cod
on curly kale and bacon

2 rashers smoked bacon, cut
into strips
50g butter
500ml water
salt and pepper
200g kale, picked and washed
24 new potatoes, Charlotte if
possible
150g melted butter
4 200-250g cod fillets, trimmed and
pin boned
extra virgin olive oil
4 tsp aïoli
4 slices Parma ham (optional)
for the crust
1 cup of brioche crumbs
small bunch of coriander leaves
$1/4$ tsp ground turmeric
$1/4$ tsp ground coriander
pinch of chilli powder
$1/2$ tsp minced garlic

Sauté bacon in hot pan until crisp and set aside. Heat butter and water, sprinkle with sea salt and ground white pepper, add kale, put lid on and cook for 5–7 minutes until tender. Drain and add bacon, set aside and keep warm.

Slice potatoes very thinly using a mandolin, leaving skin on. Place sliced potatoes in melted butter and mix through well. Season lightly with salt and pepper, then, using a non-stick frying pan, arrange the slices overlapping to form a circular pile, perhaps 3 slices high. Place pan on stove and gently cook. Brown on one side, then, after about 5 minutes, carefully turn potatoes over and place pan into a hot oven (200°C/gas mark 6) for a further 5–7 minutes to cook through. Carefully lift out on to a warm plate.

For the crust: place all ingredients in a processor, whizz up to fine crumbs and set aside.

Heat a frying pan, add a smearing of olive oil. Sprinkle a little sea salt over the skin of cod fillets, place skin side down in a hot pan and cook for about 3–5 minutes, until skin starts to crispen. Turn cod over and place pan into a hot oven for about 5 minutes. Remove from oven, and sprinkle some of the crust over the skin. Place under the grill to brown lightly.

To serve, have a warm plate with potatoes ready, pile some of the kale and bacon on top of the potato. Carefully place the cod on top of the kale and drizzle some extra virgin olive oil around the plate. Place a small spoonful of aïoli on top of fish and serve.

For a final flourish top with a slice of Parma ham, very thin, deep-fried very quickly in oil that has been heated up to 170°C. Lift out and drain on kitchen paper before draping it over fish.

Roast Perthshire partridge

on a celeriac and apple rösti, with a casserole of its thigh meat and a heather-infused jus

4 partridges
2 litres chicken stock
1 onion, sliced
1 carrot, sliced
1 leek, sliced
2 sticks of celery, sliced
a sprig of thyme
1/2 cup dried cep
1 glass of Madeira
a nice sprig of wild heather
250g button mushrooms
250ml double cream
1 tbsp each of parsley and
tarragon, chopped

1 celeriac, peeled
1 potato, peeled
2 Granny Smith apples,
peeled
150ml melted butter
100g filo pastry
2 tbsp clarified butter
25g butter, chopped

First prepare partridge: remove legs, separate thighs from drumsticks, take off wing bones, trim birds to leave just the 'crown', i.e. breasts on the bone. Place all the trimmings and drumsticks into a deep pan, add 1 1/2 litres of chicken stock, sliced vegetables, thyme and dried ceps, bring to the boil, skim and simmer slowly for about 2 hours. Strain twice, once through a muslin cloth. Pour into a clean pan and add a good glass of Madeira. Set over heat and reduce down to about 1/2 litre, correct seasoning and set aside. This will be your jus. Add sprig of heather to infuse.

Place thighs in a pan and cover with remainder of chicken stock. Bring to the boil and simmer gently with a lid on for about 30 minutes, until meat is cooked and falling off the bone. Remove thighs from stock and cool.

Flake off meat. Chop and sauté button mushrooms, remove and add to meat. Deglaze pan with a splash of Madeira, add strained cooking liquor and reduce down to a syrup. Add cream, chopped tarragon and parsley and boil till well blended, then stir in meat and mushrooms. Set aside.

For the rösti: grate celeriac, potato and apple, place into clean cloth, sprinkle a little salt over, then squeeze out moisture, leaving a well-mixed pile of grated vegetables. Stir in melted butter and add a little ground pepper. Heat 4 blini non-stick pans, place a pile of mixture into each hot pan and pat down. Colour gently over heat, then place in a hot oven (200°C/gas mark 6) for about 7 minutes. Remove, turn over, lightly colour the other side and then place on wire rack to drain and cool.

Make small filo pastry baskets that will hold the casserole of thigh meat, lightly brown them in oven (at 170°C/gas mark 3) and keep warm. Heat a sauté pan, add a little clarified butter, then place partridge crowns breast down into the pan and coat with the hot butter. Brown lightly all over, then cover birds with loose foil and place into hot oven for about 8 minutes. Remove, check and allow to rest.

When ready to serve, warm röstis gently, heat up casserole and warm filo baskets. Warm up heather-infused jus, strain out heather, reboil jus and correct seasoning, whisking in a few pieces of cold butter. Remove partridge breasts from bone. Place röstis on each plate, along with filo basket. Fill basket with casserole, arrange 2 breasts on each rösti, coat with a little jus and offer more in a gravy boat. Serve with a purée of root vegetables.

Iced praline and Amaretto soufflé

for the praline

125g flaked almonds
150g castor sugar
juice of ½ lemon

for the soufflé

100g castor sugar
4 tbsp water
4 egg yolks
350ml double cream
50ml Amaretto
6 egg whites
1 dessertspoon castor sugar

For the praline: warm flaked almonds in a moderate oven for about 10 minutes to lightly colour and dry. Heat castor sugar in a heavy-bottomed pan with a few drops of water and squeezed lemon juice. Raise heat and lightly caramelise, stir in almond flakes and pour on to a tray lined with parchment paper. Leave to cool and set.

Break up with a rolling pin then whizz up in a processor to a fine crumb. Store in an airtight jar.

For the soufflé: place sugar and water into pan, heat to a soft ball stage (160°C), pour into a mixing bowl, cool for a minute then add the yolks. Whisk at high speed to a stiff sabayon that's light and creamy. Lightly whip cream and Amaretto – not too thick.

Whisk egg whites with a dessertspoon of sugar to meringue consistency. Add half praline mix to sabayon, then cream. Mix lightly, then gently fold in egg whites.

Fold a piece of double-thickness parchment paper around each ramekin so that there is a 2 inch lip above the rim. Attach firmly with tape or an elastic band.

Pour the mixture into prepared ramekins. Sprinkle more praline over top and sides and freeze for 2 hours.

Remove and serve with almond biscuits.

Peter Jukes
The Cellar

I have very clear memories of my car journey, over nineteen years ago now, from Castle Combe in Wiltshire to Anstruther. I was driving north to view a restaurant for sale that had been recommended by a friend. It was an eventful day: word that HMS Sheffield had been lost in the Falklands was on the news as I approached the southern Lake District in my much-loved Citroën Pallas. I left the northern Lakes in an identical-looking – but in fact different, hired version – of my car (I had crashed my own car into the central reservation!). I arrived in Anstruther on a dreich, late winter's evening, wondering if I should just turn round and head for familiar Edinburgh, but I didn't. I viewed the restaurant and left not much later the proud, lucky owner of the Cellar – one of the most atmospheric restaurants I'd ever seen – with its open fires, natural stone walls and beamed ceilings.

Today, the Cellar is famed for its seafood, fine wines and relaxed, friendly, "natural" atmosphere. The cooking is simple, based on impeccable raw ingredients, chosen in season – simply and freshly cooked. Natural cooking in its simplest form.

The success I've enjoyed here is well-documented by the guides, but I sometimes feel visiting chefs come here and wonder "what's all the fuss about?". Too many chefs pay too much attention to inappropriate marriages of items – over-complication of dishes – and give scant attention to seasons of seafood. Mussels are at their best in autumn and winter; crabs from May to November; lobster should be bought with great care in high summer as no amount of skill can compensate for the watery, squidgy claws you get after the lobster has just cast its shell. Attention to detail is crucial.

Cooking and eating out is something to be enjoyed and is all about being relaxed and in the right frame of mind.

I've enjoyed a lot of success here in Scotland and, whilst I'll never make my fortune, I've met some wonderful, appreciative people who go away and spread the word about the much elevated level of cooking to be found around Scotland.

Mussels

with a shallot, thyme and garlic broth

4 shallots, finely chopped
2 cloves of garlic, crushed
1 small carrot, in thin strips
1 small leek, in thin strips
50g butter
1kg mussels
175ml white wine
175ml vegetable stock
50ml double cream
Maldon sea salt
black pepper
a few sprigs of fresh thyme

In a saucepan, gently sweat shallots, garlic, carrot and leek in butter. Do not allow to colour.

Add cleaned mussels, white wine and vegetable stock and shake pan. Put lid on to steam mussels open. Add double cream. Season with Maldon salt, black pepper, and sprigs of thyme. Serve after 2–3 minutes, when all mussels have opened (discard any still closed after this time).

Grilled halibut

with bacon, pine nuts, greens and mash

$^1/_2$ small savoy cabbage
1 sweetheart cabbage
$^1/_2$ kg Maris Piper potatoes
50g butter
olive oil
nutmeg
4 rashers smoked bacon, chopped
250g clarified butter
50g pine nuts
salt and pepper
4 x 175g halibut fillet
juice of 1 lemon
Maldon salt
1 tbsp breadcrumbs
green vegetables: snow peas,
green beans, broccoli

Cut cabbage into strips, cook in boiling water for 30 seconds. Refresh under cold water. Squeeze out water.

Boil potatoes until just cooked. Drain off water and ensure they are dry by putting them in oven for 2 minutes. Beat in butter and a splash of olive oil. Add nutmeg, to taste.

Cook diced bacon in clarified butter. Add pine nuts and colour slightly. Add cabbage. Season and keep warm.

Place halibut on tray, after seasoning with lemon juice and Maldon salt. Place breadcrumbs on top of halibut.

Cook halibut for about 4–5 minutes at 200°C/gas mark 6.

Place cabbage mix on plate with mash. Serve halibut on top. Pour around juices from pan.

Accompany with assorted green vegetables.

Seared tuna

with cracked coriander, milled black pepper, leaves and niçoise dressing

for the niçoise dressing
100ml extra virgin olive oil
3 shallots, finely chopped
juice of 1 lemon
$^1/_2$ clove of garlic, crushed
1 tbsp chopped black olives or olive paste
$^1/_2$ tbsp (tiny) capers
3 anchovy fillets, finely chopped

for the tuna
100g green beans
a selection of salad leaves
Maldon salt   black pepper
1 tbsp extra virgin olive oil
juice of 1 lemon
$^1/_2$ red onion, finely sliced
16 cherry tomatoes, halved
4 x 175g tuna loin steaks
1 tbsp cracked coriander seeds

For the niçoise dressing (this is best made in advance and will keep in the fridge for a couple of weeks): warm olive oil and shallots over a low heat – do not allow shallots to fry. Take off the heat and add all the other ingredients to oil and allow to cool.

Cook and cool green beans. Chop into 1cm pieces. Season salad leaves with Maldon salt, black pepper, olive oil and half the lemon juice. Add beans, sliced red onion and cherry tomatoes.

Evenly divide between 4 plates by placing in middle of plate, leaving a perimeter for the dressing.

Season tuna with crushed coriander, salt and pepper.

Sear tuna on a hot griddle pan. The tuna is best served pink in the middle – this is achieved by cooking each side for 1 minute. The tuna can be cooked for longer, if you prefer.

Once cooked, squeeze remaining lemon juice on fish, place on top of salad and spoon dressing round the edge of the plate and serve. The dish may be made more substantial by adding boiled baby new potatoes.

Praline parfait

for the praline

75g hazelnuts
100g castor sugar
25g flaked almonds

for the parfait

275ml double cream
3–4 medium egg whites
100g icing sugar
100g crushed praline

for the coulis

500g fresh or frozen berries
275ml water
125g castor sugar
75ml crème de cassis
fruit and berries, to garnish

For the praline (make a day in advance to make sure it sets and cools properly): roast hazelnuts in a medium-hot oven (180–220°C/gas mark 4–7) for 5–10 minutes or until skins have all split and come away from nuts. Remove from oven and allow to cool slightly, then place in a kitchen cloth and rub together to remove skins.

In a heavy-based saucepan, heat and melt sugar to caramel, being careful not to overcook the sugar as this will make the praline bitter. The caramel should be golden brown in colour.

Add hazelnuts and flaked almond to sugar and stir in. Speed is now of the essence due to the fact that caramel will be starting to set and will then be more difficult to turn out of pan. Turn out praline on to a tinfoiled baking tray, and allow to cool and set for about 3 hours. If not being used, put praline into an airtight container.

Crush the praline using a food processor (or by hand, with a rolling pin or kitchen mallet).

For the parfait: whip double cream until it forms soft peaks. It is important not to over-whip it. Keep it as light as possible. Place icing sugar and egg whites in a glass or stainless-steel bowl (make sure you don't use plastic when using egg whites, as they will not whip). The egg whites will take between 5 and 10 minutes to whip to a stiff peak consistency. Then fold the eggs through the cream, add the praline and fold through.

Spoon mixture in to a clingfilm-lined 25cm terrine mould. Smooth the top of the parfait and knock the base of the parfait mould on a bench – this helps remove any air bubbles. Cover with clingfilm and place in freezer – ideally overnight.

For the coulis: place fruit, cassis, water and castor sugar in pan and bring to boil. Allow to simmer for 20 minutes. Blitz in food processor. Sieve if required.

To serve, cut parfait into 1–2cm slices (depending on appetite). Serve on pool of fruit coulis and garnish with fresh fruit and berries of your choice. Before serving, sprinkle plate and parfait with some of the remaining praline powder. Any excess can be stored in an airtight container – it's great with vanilla ice cream.

Patricia and Tim Martin
Scarista House

Patricia: Scarista House is a small hotel as well as a restaurant, so it's quite a departure from what we've done in the past. Although we aim for traditional comfort in the rooms, our cooking is modern and fresh.

Tim: Like all Scottish restaurants we have access to fantastic ingredients, but there is a sense of immediacy here which we really relish. The sea is only a few yards away, and our shellfish supplier calls us from his boat to tell us what's coming in and to ask us what we want. There are sheep and cattle grazing all around the house, and game on the hill across the bay.

Patricia: We're growing more and more of our own leaves and herbs, too. We can order a lot of our supplies, like cheese or tea and coffee, by telephone or over the internet, but organic vegetables and salads can be a real problem. Our local shop helps us out with a twice-weekly order from Glasgow, but this is an island, so everything has to come in by plane or ferry.

Tim: We ran a restaurant together before, but it was a very different set-up. For ten years we had the restaurant franchise at the Henry Wood Hall in London, catering for musicians who were rehearsing or recording classical music. Cooking was my first career. I cooked in my father's pub in South Wales, then went to London to cook for Justin de Blank, who ran restaurants and delis. After that, I worked in publishing and television for a few years, but I knew that I really wanted to work for myself and get back to cooking.

Patricia: I'm from Northern Ireland, and studied music at Queen's University. I learnt piano and violin, but decided to work in arts administration. I was with the Royal Philharmonic, Opera Factory and the Orchestra of the Age of Enlightenment before I started cooking with Tim. We do sometimes miss the buzz of being able to pop out to a concert or a film, but when you step out of the door and see three miles of shell-sand beach, well, you can't beat that, can you?

Malfatti of langoustines and crowdie

with prawn butter sauce

for the pasta

350g pasta flour
salt
2 eggs
5 egg yolks

for the malfatti

16 large langoustines
70g crowdie
2 tsp lemon juice
tabasco sauce
salt and black pepper
100g fresh pasta
flour for dusting (preferably
pasta flour)
1 tbsp finely snipped chives or
chervil

for the prawn butter sauce

3 shallots, finely chopped
1 medium carrot, finely
chopped
shells, heads and
claws from langoustines
$\frac{1}{2}$ tbsp groundnut oil
a few sprigs of tarragon or
6 young lovage leaves
a pinch of saffron threads and
some to decorate
200ml dry white wine
100ml brandy
2 tbsp tomato purée
250g unsalted butter
400ml fish stock
100ml double cream and
some to decorate
salt

For the pasta: blitz flour and salt. Add eggs and then egg yolks and process to a sticky lump. Remove from machine and knead into ball. Cut into four. Clingfilm. Rest in fridge for 1 hour. Use quarter for recipe. (Malfatti — an Italian term meaning 'badly made', are slightly irregularly formed pasta parcels.)

For the malfatti: briefly cook langoustines in boiling water (for no more than a minute or a little longer if they are frozen), then peel them and keep heads, claws and shells for sauce. Keep back the 8 best-looking langoustine tails. Blitz the rest with the crowdie, chives, lemon juice and 4 drops of tabasco. Season mix with black pepper. Using a pasta machine, roll out pasta to the thinnest setting and lay strips of pasta on a well-floured work surface. Cut strips into 8 postcard-size pieces. Put a good dessertspoon of langoustine stuffing into the middle of each piece of pasta, and top it with a langoustine tail. Brush edges of pasta with water and fold over to enclose stuffing, pressing out any air and sealing edges. You can trim edges of each parcel with a knife or a ravioli wheel if you want. Lay parcels on a tray well dusted with flour.

For the prawn butter sauce: in a sauté pan, sweat shallots, carrot and chopped langoustine shells, heads and claws in a little groundnut oil for 5 minutes. Add tarragon or lovage and let it wilt. Stir in saffron. Pour in wine and reduce it by three-quarters. Add brandy and ignite it. Shake pan until the flames die down, then stir in tomato purée. Blitz mixture in a processor or blender, then return it to the pan. Add butter and let it no more than melt over a low flame. Set pan aside and let it cool, but not so much that butter congeals. Line a bowl with a 25cm square of doubled muslin. Ladle 2 or 3 tablespoons of the mixture at a time into the muslin and – wearing clean, but not new, rubber gloves to protect yourself from the heat – gather up the corners of the muslin, squeezing and twisting it to force out the unctuous, highly flavoured prawn butter. You can keep it in the fridge for a day or finish the sauce straight away. Reduce fish stock to about 2 tablespoons. Dissolve prawn butter in it, then pour in cream and bubble it to reduce it slightly, so that it coats the spoon. Season it with salt if necessary and keep it warm.

To serve, have ready a wide pan, not too deep, of boiling water. As your guests go to the table, slip malfatti into it. Warm sauce and put a couple of tablespoons on to each warmed plate. Lift malfatti with a slotted spoon and let them drain before putting them on to the plates and covering them with the rest of the sauce. Decorate them with a dribble of double cream and 3 or 4 saffron strands.

Patricia and Tim Martin
Scarista House

Sound of Harris lobster
split and grilled with green peppercorn sauce and sage

4 live lobsters, about 500g each,
preferably from the Sound of Harris
1 dessertspoon green peppercorns
400ml fish stock
150g unsalted butter
200ml white Burgundy
100ml double cream
salt
12 fresh sage leaves
25g butter

Treat lobsters kindly. To kill them, wrap them carefully in damp seaweed or newspaper and freeze them for up to 5 hours. Thaw them for an hour or so, then split them lengthways with a large, strong, sharp knife. Crack the claws.

Pound green peppercorns to a gritty paste with a pestle and mortar or with the end of a rolling pin in the bottom of a mug.

Reduce fish stock to about 3 tablespoons.

Melt butter and let peppercorns infuse in it over a very low heat, without it bubbling, for 3 minutes, then add wine and simmer mixture for a short while to homogenise it and reduce wine.

Add reduced stock and cream and bubble sauce until it has thickened enough to coat a spoon. Season it with salt, if necessary.

Grill lobsters under a very high heat until shells are completely reddened. Fry sage leaves to a crisp in butter and serve lobster with leaves on top, coated with a little sauce and with the rest of the sauce in a sauceboat.

Patricia and Tim Martin
Scarista House

Supreme of corn-fed guinea fowl

with raspberry and rowanberry gravy

4 supremes of corn-fed
guinea fowl, skin on
salt and black pepper
1 tbsp of eau-de-vie de
framboise sauvage
200ml red wine (Merlot is best)
2 tbsps crème de framboise
1 sprig of thyme
3 shallots, peeled and sliced
300ml veal stock
1 scant tbsp of Moniack
rowanberry jelly
75g unsalted butter

Season supremes and sear them on both sides on a very hot, ribbed griddle. Lay them on a tray sprinkled with framboise and roast them at 200°C/gas mark 6 for 25 minutes.

Put wine and crème de framboise in a pan with thyme and shallots and reduce liquid by half. Add stock and bubble it for up to 10 minutes to reduce it further. Skim surface as necessary.

Whisk jelly, strain liquid through a fine sieve and put it back on the heat in a clean pan. Whisk in cubed, chilled butter. Season sauce and add a little more jelly if it is too sharp. If your stock is any good, you should have a purplish, limpid, slightly musky but sweet-tasting and highly flavoured sauce with which to surround each guinea fowl supreme.

Patricia and Tim Martin
Scarista House

Chocolate roulade

with white chocolate and mint ice cream and hot bitter chocolate sauce

for the roulade

100g good quality plain chocolate, such as Valrhona
3 large free-range eggs, separated
100g castor sugar
2 tbsp hot water
icing sugar, to serve
250ml whipped cream, to serve

for the white chocolate and mint ice cream

280ml single cream
8 fresh mint leaves
3 egg yolks
75g castor sugar
125g white chocolate
280ml double cream

for the bitter chocolate sauce

50g cocoa powder
75g castor sugar
175ml water
10g softened butter

For the roulade: pre-heat oven to 190°C. Line a shallow tin approximately 25 x 35 cm with baking parchment. Melt chocolate in a bain-marie set over a low heat. Beat egg yolks and sugar together until they are thick, pale and creamy and then add hot water. Continue to beat for a few seconds until well mixed. Mix melted chocolate into egg and sugar mixture. Beat the egg whites until they form soft peaks and then fold them into chocolate mixture. Pour mixture into tin. Bake for 5–10 minutes or until it is springy to the touch. Leave to cool in the tin.

For the white chocolate and mint ice-cream: bring single cream to the boil, remove from heat and add mint leaves. Beat egg yolks and sugar together with a fork. Add single cream and mint leaves and mix well. Pour into a bain-marie and stir constantly until mixture thickens enough to coat the back of a spoon. This could take up to 10 or 15 minutes. Remove from heat and leave to cool. When cool, strain to remove mint leaves.

In another bain-marie melt white chocolate and then beat it into mint custard. Chill.

Lightly whip double cream and fold it into chilled mint and white chocolate mixture. Pour this mixture into an ice-cream machine and churn it until it is frozen.

For the bitter chocolate sauce: combine cocoa, sugar and water in a saucepan and whisk until they are well amalgamated. Bring to the boil over a low heat, whisking continuously, and simmer for a couple of minutes. Whisk in butter, a little at a time and cook for another 2 minutes. To serve, flip the roulade on to a sheet of baking parchment, dusted with icing sugar. Spread it with whipped cream and roll it up using the paper. Dust roulade with more icing sugar. Put a slice of roulade on each of the 4 plates.

Using 2 tablespoons dipped in hot water, make quenelles of ice cream and put one next to each slice of roulade.

Dribble hot chocolate sauce over both the roulade and ice cream.

Wendy and Don Matheson – Owners
Charlie Lockley – Chef
Boath House

After several years of extensive renovations, Boath House, a historic Grade A listed mansion house, opened its doors four years ago. We had bought the house as a virtual ruin and were anxious to keep the relaxed country-house feel in spite of the makeover. We were keen to avoid a traditional 'hotel' image which we felt was too commercial for our personal vision for Boath House. Our approach to the decor and furniture is very eclectic, and this helps to enhance the relaxed atmosphere of the place. We both love contemporary art, and the house is full of the work of local artists and craftsmen, some of it for sale.

After renovating the house, we turned our attention to revitalising the 20 acre garden, which included re-stocking the Trout Lake. This year's project is to reinstate the Victorian walled garden where we currently house our own kitchen garden which already supplies the kitchen with most of the organically grown vegetables, soft fruits and herbs over the summer and autumn months.

Wendy initially did the cooking, but on meeting Charlie and talking to him about his experience and ideas, we realised he shared our aspirations and commitment to quality. He's been with us ever since, and it's worked wonderfully. His quiet and unfailingly courteous manner disguises a true passion for cooking, along with an unerring instinct for unusual combinations of food. The cooking style at Boath House is based on using the abundance of local produce, much of it organic. We have a five course, daily changing menu, and the food is about the marriage of flavour combination and uncomplicated preparation. As Charlie says, "let the ingredients do the talking". We try to keep the menu simple, no essays, just reflecting the fact that it is good food, simply prepared. We have a great team at Boath House, a wonderful working environment, and we love working with people. The emphasis is on good food, good wine, and relaxation. Our spa facilities offer Ayurvedic treatments, sauna and Jacuzzi, helping to ensure that each guest is given every opportunity to feel pampered and totally relaxed.

Wendy and Don Matheson & Charlie Lockley
Boath House

Confit of salmon
with a watercress butter

4 x 150g salmon fillets, evenly
trimmed
40g sea salt
20g castor sugar
5g white peppercorns crushed
zest of 1 lime
zest of 1 lemon
500ml olive oil
3 cloves of garlic, whole
1 bay leaf
1 sprig of tarragon
1 sprig of basil
1 sprig of chervil
8 baby aubergines, halved
salt and pepper
1 sprig of thyme
12 baby fennel, trimmed
20 asparagus spears
for the sauce
100ml white chicken stock
50g watercress
50g unsalted butter, diced
4 tsp caviar (optional)
4 sprigs of chervil

The day before, mix together salt, sugar, peppercorns and both zests. Rub into both sides of salmon fillets and wrap in clingfilm. Place on a tray and put in fridge for 4 hours.

Then unwrap salmon and wash under cold water to remove salt mix. Pat dry. Replace on tray and cover with olive oil. Add 2 cloves of garlic and herbs (except thyme) and leave in fridge for at least 12 hours. When ready, remove salmon from oil and pat dry.

Sieve the oil into heavy-bottomed pan (large enough to take salmon fillets in a single layer).

Meanwhile, place baby aubergines in a double layer of tinfoil. Season. Add remaining clove of garlic and sprig of thyme. Add a little olive oil. Seal foil so that it looks like a Cornish pastie. Place in oven for 40 minutes (190°C/gas mark 5) and cook until soft.

In a separate pot, cook fennel and asparagus in salted water until tender and refresh in ice-cold water.

Bring chicken stock to the boil in a pan and add watercress. Season and cover. Cook for 4 minutes. Liquidise then pass through a fine sieve into a clean pan. Whisk in diced butter. Check seasoning.

Put pan with olive oil on to a low heat. When oil temperature reaches 50°C, place fillets in oil. Leave for 15–20 minutes. When cooked, remove from oil and gently pat dry. Leave to rest for a few minutes.

Warm sauce, place in middle of plate, and pile warmed vegetables on top. Place salmon on top and garnish with caviar and chervil to finish.

Wendy and Don Matheson & Charlie Lockley
Boath House

Pea soup

with foie gras raviolis and white truffle oil

40g butter
75g lightly smoked bacon
250g onions, finely diced
75g potatoes, finely diced
1 clove of garlic, roughly chopped
600ml white chicken stock
400g peas (fresh or frozen)
salt and pepper
1 tsp fresh tarragon, chopped

for the chicken mousse

100g raw chicken breast, diced
1 egg white
75ml double cream
salt and pepper

for the ravioli

275g pasta flour
$^1/_4$ tsp salt
2 whole eggs
3 egg yolks
1 tbsp olive oil
100g foie gras, in small dice
1 tsp fresh chopped chives
salt and pepper
100g chicken mousse
1 egg (for egg wash)

for the white truffle oil

50ml milk
50ml crème fraîche
a few drops white truffle oil (to taste)
25g unsalted butter, diced

Gently heat butter in a large pan. Add bacon, onions and potatoes. Cook for a couple of minutes then add garlic and cook for another minute.

Pour in white chicken stock and bring to the boil. Cover and simmer until potatoes are soft. Add peas, bring back to the boil. Remove from heat. Add salt, pepper and tarragon. Liquidise soup and pass through fine sieve. Adjust seasoning, if required. Chill until ready (to keep colour).

For the chicken mousse: chill mixing bowl. Add diced breast of chicken and blend for 30 seconds. Add egg white, and slowly add double cream. Season and place in fridge.

For the ravioli: sieve flour and salt into blender. In a bowl, whisk whole eggs, yolks and olive oil and slowly add to flour. Mix until dough comes together. Turn out on to lightly floured surface and knead for about 10 minutes until smooth (no cracks). Wrap in clingfilm and chill for 2 hours. Divide into 4 and pass through pasta machine twice on all settings.

Fold diced foie gras, chives, salt and pepper into chicken mousse. Put into a small-nozzled piping bag.

On a lightly floured surface, lay out 4 sheets of pasta at a time and pipe a small amount of mousse into the middle of each sheet. Brush with egg wash and lay another sheet of pasta on top, pressing out air. Repeat. With a small, round pastry cutter (3cm) cut out ravioli and crimp edges for a firm seal.

Gently heat soup. Meanwhile, drop raviolis into boiling salted water for 2 minutes.

For the white truffle oil: heat milk, crème fraîche and white truffle oil. Mix in butter. Season and blitz with hand-blender until frothy.

To serve, pour soup into bowls. Add ravioli. Spoon over a little of froth.

Young grouse

with sweet potato purée and aged balsamic glaze

for the purée

750g orange sweet potato
2 tbsp peanut oil
salt and pepper
50g butter

for the grouse

4 young grouse
4 large sprigs of thyme
2 tbsp peanut oil
8 slices streaky bacon
20g butter

for garlic crisps

6 cloves of garlic
1 tbsp peanut oil

for the vegetables

250g savoy cabbage, shredded
20g butter
50g shallots, chopped

for the glaze

120ml aged balsamic vinegar
1 juniper berry, crushed
1 clove of garlic, crushed
1 sprig of thyme
60ml grouse stock (reduced)

Scrub sweet potatoes. Pour 2 tablespoons of peanut oil into large roasting tray and heat. Add potatoes and brush lightly with heated oil. Place in oven (200°C/gas mark 6) for 1–1½ hours or until soft. Remove and leave to cool a little. Pat dry, place into a bowl and mash. Pass through a fine sieve. Season. Add 50g butter. Put on one side.

Place a sprig of thyme in each grouse then tie and truss and season. Heat 2 tablespoons of peanut oil in a pan and seal birds on all sides until nicely browned. Place 2 slices of bacon on each breast and rub with 5g of butter. Place in oven for 15–20 minutes (200°C/gas mark 6).

When ready, remove from oven and take off string. Leave to rest in a warm place for 10 minutes.

Peel 6 garlic cloves and slice thinly. Bring a pan of salted water to the boil and blanch garlic. Refresh in cold water. Repeat process twice.

Pat dry garlic slices and then fry for 10 minutes in remaining peanut oil. Drain on to kitchen paper.

Blanch cabbage in salted boiling water for 1 minute, then drain. Heat 20g butter in a pan and add shallots. Cook for 1 minute and add cabbage. Cook for another minute, season and serve crisp.

Put vinegar, juniper berry, garlic, thyme, salt and pepper into pan. Bring to boil and add stock. Reduce until you have a nice syrupy consistency. Then sieve through muslin.

When everything is ready, heat potato purée – cook a little to remove any liquid. Place a small mound of purée on plate, add cabbage. Carve breast from birds and place on cabbage. Arrange legs and bacon on top. Scatter garlic crisps and drizzle glaze.

Wendy and Don Matheson & Charlie Lockley
Boath House

Chocolate truffle torte

with raspberry sorbet

1 thin layer of Genoise sponge (25cm)
250g fresh raspberries
250ml double cream
1 tsp vanilla essence
200g dark chocolate (70% cocoa solids, chopped)
2 tbsp liquid glucose
50g unsalted butter, diced
sprigs of mint
icing sugar, to dust

for the sorbet
100g castor sugar
100ml water
250g fresh raspberries

(Makes 25cm diameter cake.
Serves 12)

Line cake tin with clingfilm. Place sponge on bottom. Pulp raspberries and spread evenly over sponge.

Put cream and vanilla into a pan and slowly bring to the boil, then pour over chocolate pieces. Add liquid glucose and butter and whisk together. Pour mixture over sponge and raspberry pulp and place in fridge. Remove 1 hour before serving.

For the sorbet: place sugar and water in pan and bring slowly to the boil. Simmer for 5 minutes.

Place raspberries in liquidiser, pour over stock syrup and blitz for 30 seconds. Pass through a fine nylon sieve and leave to cool. Once cooled, churn in ice-cream machine and freeze.

To serve, place a slice of chocolate torte and a scoop of sorbet on to plate. Garnish with mint and dust with icing sugar.

Donald McInnes, Andrew Costley, Laurent Labede and Bruce Boyd

Lochgreen House

Donald: I came to Lochgreen from Cameron House earlier this year, as Executive Chef. One of the great things about working here is that it's not a one man show – there are four of us – and we all work to very high standards. As soon as I met Andrew, I knew we'd get on; we do, and we make a very good team. From the age of ten, I knew I wanted to cook – it's a good profession to be in these days, a growing art. I enjoy the freedom of cooking what I like to eat, and it's very gratifying when people like the food I cook. Food has evolved so much. It used to be about impressing the plate, but now it's much more about impressing the palate. Food is very visual, but it's got to be about the taste too.

Andrew: I always knew that I wanted to be a chef. I loved helping out and being involved – even if it was just peeling the potatoes. I started working for Costley & Costley when I was at college and got so involved that I didn't find time to study, so I dropped out and learned on the job. When we took on the Cochrane Inn, I spent the first year there with my dad, before coming to Lochgreen. This is very much a family-run business. My mum is very involved; she and my mother-in-law are responsible for all the interior decoration and the flower-arrangements. And my father-in-law is in charge of banqueting at Brig O'Doon. I like being hands on – cooking is what I'm good at and what I love, and this is a great place to do it. At Lochgreen, we aim to be the best and to build on our reputation for fine-dining and comfort.

Laurent: I was brought up in this business. My father ran a Michelin starred restaurant outside Toulouse. Most of my family are either chefs or waiters and food was always very important. I trained for seven years as a chef and worked in lots of places, including Tahiti. I knew that I needed to learn English, so I came to Scotland and fell in love with the country and a Scottish woman, and stayed! I love working here. We are young, and we all want to do the best, and to keep the guests happy.

Bruce: After leaving the army, I got on a course at Glasgow Food Tech. Being a pastry chef is a real speciality; the money is good and there are lots of chances to travel. I like the fact that I work with sweet-smelling ingredients – I wouldn't like to come home smelling of fish! I worked at Gleneagles on and off for ten years, with breaks to work in New Zealand and Cyprus, and I've done pastry demonstrations all over the world. My job here is Executive Pastry Chef, which is a new post with opportunities for development – that's the big attraction as well as the great reputation of the company.

Donald McInnes, Andrew Costley, Laurent Labede and Bruce Boyd
Lochgreen House

Cep omelette

with seared Arran Bay scallops and langoustine dressing

3 eggs
1 pinch of fine salt
pepper
50g ceps, finely diced
40g unsalted butter

for the filling

25g butter
1 banana shallot, finely diced
50g ceps, sliced
salt and pepper

for the dressing

5g coriander seeds
5g mustard seeds
1 star anise
1 cardamom pod
1 banana shallot, finely chopped
100ml olive oil
1 litre clarified langoustine stock
50ml Noilly Prat
25g balsamic vinegar
salt and pepper
2 fresh hand-dived scallops
cleaned and coral removed
1 sprig of chervil, to garnish

(Serves one)

Beat eggs and season. Gently fry mushrooms in half of the butter, then add to egg mix. Melt remaining butter in omelette pan and cook omelette until set.

For the filling: melt butter and add shallot and ceps. Cook until soft. Season to taste.

Place omelette on a board, add the cep mixture in the middle and fold into a neat parcel.

For the dressing: add coriander, mustard seed, star anise and cardamom to a hot dry pan and crush to release flavour. Add shallot with 5ml olive oil, stirring quickly. Add langoustine stock and reduce by two-thirds.

Add Noilly Prat and balsamic vinegar. Reduce again for about 2-3 minutes. Finally strain through a fine sieve and whisk in the remaining olive oil. Season with salt and pepper to taste.

Slice each scallop straight through the middle – the side you have sliced is the presentation side once it is fried.

To serve, place neat omelette parcel in centre of plate. Sear scallops and place neatly on top. Warm dressing, drizzle around and finish with sprigs of chervil.

Medallions of veal

served with gateau of oxtail and creamed celeriac, red wine and morel sauce

for the braised oxtail

2 oxtails
570ml red wine
50ml red wine vinegar
2 bulbs of garlic
salt and pepper
1 carrot, chopped
1 onion, chopped
1 stick of celery, chopped
1 leek, chopped
2 sprigs of fresh thyme
50g soft brown sugar
1 litre brown chicken stock

for the celeriac and potato purée

720g celeriac, peeled
300g potatoes (King Edward or
Desirée)
150g butter
150ml double cream
salt, pepper and grated fresh
nutmeg

for the potato galette

2 Maris Piper potatoes, peeled
clarified butter
600g veal: 4 medallions per person
(trimmed and bone cleaned),
seasoned
1 tbsp vegetable oil
salt and pepper

For the braised oxtail: marinade in red wine and red wine vinegar, with garlic, chopped vegetables, thyme and sugar for 24 hours, turning maybe twice. Once marinated, remove nuggets of meat and seal in a hot pan. Add to a roasting or deep tray with all the marinade liquor and vegetables. Add brown chicken stock. Bring to the boil, cover the tray with tinfoil and braise in a very low oven (150°C/gas mark 2) for around 3-4 hours, checking occasionally. The meat is ready when it almost falls from the bone when touched.

For the celeriac and potato purée: cook celeriac in lightly salted water for approximately 10 minutes and drain. Pass celeriac through a fine sieve. Cook potato in lightly salted water for approximately 20 minutes, drain and sieve. Combine both purées, add butter and cream and mix well. Add grated nutmeg, salt and pepper to taste.

For the potato galette: cut Maris Piper potato into thin slices with a mandolin, then cut into circles with a cutter. Using a small blini or frying pan heat up a little clarified butter and arrange potato circles in pan to form a flower shape. Cook slowly for approximately 10 minutes until crisp, turning if necessary. Allow to dry on a paper towel.

Season veal medallions with salt and pepper and seal in vegetable oil in a medium-hot pan and cook for 3-4 minutes on each side. Allow to rest.

Donald McInnes, Andrew Costley, Laurent Labede and Bruce Boyd
Lochgreen House

for the red wine sauce

3 shallots, finely sliced

3 cloves of garlic

4 sprigs of thyme

5g brown sugar

50ml red wine

50ml port

1 litre veal stock

50g morel mushrooms

50ml Madeira

25g butter, diced

for the garnish

8 banana shallots, peeled and halved lengthways

1 tbsp oil

60ml red wine

30g butter

5g marmalade

For the red wine sauce: sweat off shallots, garlic and thyme. Add brown sugar to caramelise. Deglaze with red wine. Reduce. Add port and veal stock and bring to the boil. Simmer for 20 minutes, skimming frequently. Sieve through fine muslin. Run dried morels under water and squeeze dry. Soak in Madeira for minimum of 30 minutes.

Warm sauce through, add in soaked morels and whisk in diced butter.

For the garnish: heat a frying pan with a little oil, place in shallots presentation side first. Turn once coloured, add red wine, marmalade and butter.

Cook gently, spooning over the liquor.

To serve, use a metal circular mould. Place oxtail into mould, just under half full. Pipe in celeriac and potato purée. Mix and smooth with palette knife. Top with potato galette and place on one side of plate. Serve with medallions topped with shallots. Drizzle with sauce.

Donald McInnes, Andrew Costley, Laurent Labede and Bruce Boyd
Lochgreen House

Sweetbread tart with noisettes of Ayrshire lamb,

fricassée of broad bean and Madeira jus

1 saddle of lamb trimmed to two loins and wrapped in its own fat
400g lamb sweetbread
250ml milk
2 onions, chopped
2 bulbs of garlic, cut in half
salt and pepper
100ml clarified butter
100ml extra virgin olive oil
500ml Madeira
100ml cognac
100ml red wine
500ml lamb stock
15g butter
10g mustard powder
2 red peppers
170g Maris Piper/Desirée potato, cooked
1 egg
6 egg yolks
25g Parmesan, freshly grated
pinch of nutmeg
500ml double cream, reduced by half
100g broad beans, blanched and skinned
19 cloves garlic, degermed
1 bouquet garni (rosemary, thyme, bay leaves and parsley)

First of all leave lamb sweetbread to marinade for 15 hours in milk, onions, garlic, salt and pepper.

Halve red peppers, blanch, skin, deseed and purée.

Mix cooked potato with egg, egg yolks, Parmesan, puréed red pepper, nutmeg and reduced cream.

Pipe potato mixture into four 70mm metal ring and place 'tart' on baking tray. Cook for 7-8 minutes at 220°C/gas mark 7 until just becoming crispy. Once sweetbread has been marinaded, pat dry and remove skin. Fry sweetbread in clarified butter. Deglaze pan with red wine, cognac, Madeira and lamb stock. Remove sweetbread and allow to rest.

Reduce sauce. With the help of a blender, emulsify with 15g butter, olive oil, mustard powder. Check seasoning. Keep warm.

Blanch broad beans and remove skin.

Blanch all garlic cloves 3 times, changing the water each time.

Add broad beans and 12 of blanched garlic cloves to warm sauce.

Sear loins of lamb in a hot pan until fat becomes crispy. Add 7 garlic cloves with a knob of butter and bouquet garni. Place in oven at 220°C/gas mark 7 for 12-14 minutes until pink. Remove lamb and allow to rest for 5 minutes.

To serve, place potato tart in centre of plate, fill with lamb sweetbread.

Carve the loin into 5 nuggets, place around tart.

Spoon sauce over tart and a little drizzle around plate.

Donald McInnes, Andrew Costley, Laurent Labede and Bruce Boyd
Lochgreen House

Assiette of Lochgreen sweets

for the rhubarb and honey rice
40g arborio rice
160g rhubarb juice
20g clear honey
30g sugar
0.5g vanilla
4 sheets filo pastry
10g butter

For the rhubarb and honey rice: mix rice with juice. Slowly cook until thick. Fold in honey and sugar with vanilla. Allow to go cold. Put half of mix in middle of 2 sheets of filo which have been buttered. Repeat. Roll up like a sausage roll. Bake in hot oven (200°C/gas mark 6) for 10-12 minutes. Cut and serve half per cover.

Donald McInnes, Andrew Costley, Laurent Labede and Bruce Boyd
Lochgreen House

for the wild blaeberry parfait

50g blaeberries

30g sugar

2 egg yolks

juice of ½ lime

80g double cream

for the raspberry jelly

25ml stock syrup, made with 12.5g
castor sugar and 12.5ml water

45ml red wine

45ml white wine

10ml framboise

juice of ½ lemon

2 leaves of gelatine

raspberries: 8 per mould

for the oatmeal meringue

80g sugar

2 egg whites

10g pinhead oatmeal, toasted

**for the Lochgreen orchard apple
soufflé**

4 small orchard apples (Gala)

juice of ½ lemon

15g butter   15g sugar

15g flour   60ml milk

1 large egg yolk

30g apple purée

2 large egg whites

for the whisky ice cream

9 egg yolks

150g sugar

500ml milk

250ml cream

40ml Dalwhinnie whisky

4 sprigs of mint, to garnish

For the wild blaeberry parfait: place berries in a pan with sugar and boil. Purée and pass through a strainer. Allow to cool. Over a bain-marie, beat yolks until thick. Add lime juice. Semi-whip cream. Fold yolks into berries. Next fold in cream and pour into a mould. Freeze until required.

For the raspberry jelly with oatmeal meringue: make stock syrup with castor sugar and water. Boil together. Boil wines with syrup and framboise. Add lemon juice and gelatine. Allow to cool. Fill moulds with raspberries. Top up with jelly – just enough to cover berries. Allow to set. Now make the meringue. Beat the sugar and egg whites to a stiff mass. Fold in oatmeal. With a plain piping nozzle, pipe lengths of meringue. Dry overnight in oven at 80°C/gas mark ½. Once dry, cut into 0.5cm lengths and place around unmoulded jelly.

For the Lochgreen orchard apple soufflé: scoop out apple, brush with lemon juice to keep white. Mix butter with sugar and flour. Boil milk and add butter mix. Stir until thick and elastic. Add yolk and beat smooth. Add purée and allow to cool. Whip egg whites until stiff and fold into egg mix. Load back into apples and bake in hot oven for 12 minutes at 225°C/ gas mark 7. Serve immediately.

For the whisky ice cream: in a bowl, mix yolks with sugar. Boil milk and cream in a pan. Add milk/cream to yolks and mix gently. Allow to cool and add whisky. Turn in machine for 30 minutes. Freeze until required.

To serve, take the largest plate you have and place the raspberry jelly on top right. Next garnish the parfait and place bottom right. Warm the rice and stand it at the top left. Next shape and place the ice cream in centre. Garnish the ice cream with mint and, at the last minute, add the soufflé at bottom left.

The two bottom sweets complement each other as do the top two and the ice cream brings it all together. Enjoy.

Ian McNaught and Eric Brown
The Roman Camp

Eric: My family has always been involved in hotels and restaurants. My parents used to run Auchterarder House, my brother, Alan, runs the Bouzy Rouge restaurants and the youngest brother, Paul, has recently opened a new restaurant in Dunfermline. My wife, Marion and I began managing the Roman Camp in 1989, but it had been run as a country house hotel since the 1930s. The place was originally (in 1625) a hunting lodge for the Dukes of Perth, and is believed to have been built on the site of a Roman fort and the oldest soccer pitch in Scotland!

Ian: I left school with no qualifications and started a catering course. While I was at college, I got work experience with a chef called Bert Trotter at the Old Manor, Lundin Links. As soon as I got into a real kitchen, I got going. I went on to work for David Wilson at the Peat Inn and for Jimmy and Amanda Graham at Ostlers Close who were very supportive. I've been very lucky in my career – from the start I've been given the freedom to do what I wanted. That's one of the great things about the Roman Camp – I can do my own thing. I'm very committed to cooking consistently good food. I've been Head Chef here for four years and my sous chef, Darren Cotterill, has been here for the same length of time. We make a very good team.

Eric: The Roman Camp is off the main street in Callander, but it feels very secluded. Our guests see it as a place where they can escape the city, but also feel at home. Comfort is very important to what we're offering and the quality of the food is a major factor in that experience. We built an oval dining room in 1997 which gives our diners plenty of space and comfort and, in October 1999, we won three AA rosettes.

Ian: As a chef, you can never stop learning about food. I suppose the cuisine of Marco Pierre White has been a big influence on me, but I'm also inspired by what I eat in restaurants, see in the supermarket or simply by something someone says about food. I never lose my enthusiasm in this job and take pride in what we achieve.

Roasted lobster

with brandade cake, truffle vinaigrette

for the brandade cake
100g cod fillet
250ml milk
1 clove of garlic
200g mashed potatoes
1 tsp chopped chives and parsley
salt and pepper
50g flour, seasoned with salt,
pepper and pinch of cayenne
egg wash (1 egg, beaten with some
milk)
100g fresh polenta

for the truffle vinaigrette
25ml truffle juice
25ml Xeres vinegar
225ml grapeseed oil
1 tsp chopped truffle

2 plum tomatoes, skinned,
deseeded and finely chopped
2 tsp truffle oil
4 tbsp extra virgin olive oil
2 x 450g lobsters, cooked and
shelled
4 sprigs of chervil
selection of mixed salad leaves
6 tbsp olive oil
juice of ½ lemon
1 tbsp pine nuts, lightly toasted
1 smallish truffle, thinly sliced

For the brandade cake: gently poach cod in milk with garlic until just cooked, allow to go cold, then discard garlic clove. Gently flake cod and mix through mashed potato and herbs and season.

On a floured surface form 4 little pattie shapes and coat with seasoned flour, egg wash and polenta. Place in fridge to set.

For the truffle vinaigrette: whisk truffle juice and vinegar together and slowly add grapeseed oil to emulsify. Add chopped truffle, tomatoes and truffle oil and season with salt and pepper.

Place 1 tablespoon of olive oil into frying pan and heat. Fry off brandade cakes until they are crispy and have an even colour. Place in a medium-hot oven (180°C/gas mark 4) to warm through.

Heat up remaining oil and roast off lobster tails and claws. Season and keep warm.

To serve, place brandade cake in the centre of the plate, top with sliced lobster tail and 1 whole claw, then add chervil sprig to the top.

Dress salad with extra virgin olive oil and lemon juice, check seasoning. Place salad around the cake, sprinkle with pine nuts. Scatter sliced truffle and spoon over truffle vinaigrette.

Squab poached in cep broth

with foie gras tortellini

4 squab pigeons, giblets kept
50g rock salt
$1/2$ tsp thyme
400g goose fat

for the cep broth
bones and giblets from squabs
2 tbsp oil
100g each of carrot, leek, onion
and celery, roughly chopped
225g button mushrooms, sliced
75ml Madeira
1 clove of garlic
100g dried ceps
400ml chicken stock
150ml water
sprig of rosemary
$1/2$ bay leaf
4 egg whites

for the foie gras tortellini
600g 00 grade flour
2 eggs
8 egg yolks
200g chicken breast
$1/2$ tsp chopped tarragon and flat-
leaf parsley
1 whole egg
1 egg yolk
115ml double cream
200g foie gras, diced
salt and pepper
2 tbsp olive oil

for the garnish
200g spinach leaves, blanched
12 carrots, turned
12 asparagus tips, blanched and
refreshed
2 tbsp water
60g butter
200g selection of wild mushrooms
2 tbsp chives, chopped
2 tbsp cep oil
2 tbsp olive oil

Remove squab legs and trim, place on a tray, sprinkle with rock salt and thyme, refrigerate for 12 hours. Wash salt and herbs off legs and pat dry. Place in a pan with goose fat and cook at a very low heat (100°C/lowest gas mark) for 1 hour or until very tender. Make sure fat does not boil.

Bring a large pan of heavily seasoned water to the boil, blanch squab crowns for 1 minute, remove and chill in iced water for 5 minutes. Drain and place in a fridge to set. One hour will be long enough. Remove, retaining bones for the broth.

For the cep broth: chop up squab bones, heat oil in pan, brown bones then add vegetables. Cook until golden brown, add button mushrooms and cook for 2 minutes. Deglaze with Madeira, add garlic clove and dried ceps, add chicken stock and water and bring to the boil. Add rosemary and bay leaf and simmer for 45 minutes. Pass through muslin into a clean pan, allow to cook slightly. Lightly break up egg whites and add to broth. Return to a low heat, cook gently until egg whites have set and stock is clear. Pass through muslin again, check seasoning.

For the foie gras tortellini: in a blender, combine flour with eggs and add yolks, slowly, one by one – minimum 6 – to make pasta dough. Allow to rest. Cool in fridge.

Blend chicken with tarragon and parsley for 1 minute. Add egg and egg yolk, then blend for another 30 seconds, pass through a fine sieve and chill for 1 hour. Fold in double cream and diced foie gras. Season.

Shape into 12 tortellini, blanch in boiling water for 30 seconds, refresh in iced water, gently dry and toss in oil. Refrigerate until needed.

Gently poach squab breasts in cep broth; keep very pink. Warm legs through in the oven covered in foil so they don't dry out. Cook spinach in a little butter and seasoning.

Reheat vegetables in 2 tablespoons of water and 10g butter.

Sauté a selection of mushrooms in 50g butter.

Reheat tortellini in boiling salted water.

To serve, divide spinach on to 4 warm plates. Place squab legs on top, put breasts on top of legs, surround with vegetables, mushrooms and tortellini. Check seasoning. Mix chives with cep oil and olive oil and drizzle over finished dish.

Lamb best end

with basil couscous, tomato confit and aubergine purée

4 x 175–225g lamb best end
(butterfly cut so you have
4 square pieces of lamb)
4 pieces of caul fat, evenly marbled

for the basil couscous

300g couscous
150ml chicken stock
4 shallots, peeled and diced
100g butter
50g basil leaves
1 egg
salt and pepper

for the tomato confit

6 firm plum tomatoes
50g butter, 100ml olive oil
$1/2$ tsp coriander seed, crushed
1 tsp each of basil, thyme and
rosemary, chopped
1 clove of garlic, crushed

for the aubergine purée

2 aubergines, olive oil
1 clove of garlic, finely sliced
$1/2$ tsp each of thyme and rosemary,
chopped

for the aubergine crisps

$1/2$ aubergine
seasoned flour for dusting

for the pesto

50g pine kernels
50g cloves of garlic
50g fresh Parmesan, finely grated
125ml olive oil
50g basil leaves

for the lamb jus

3 tsp oil
50g each of chopped carrot, leek,
onion and celery
50ml port, 50ml brandy
1 chicken leg
500ml lamb stock
250ml chicken stock
100ml water

For the basil couscous: place couscous in bowl, pour over boiling chicken stock, mix together. Sweat off shallot in butter, add basil leaves then liquidise to a purée, fold into couscous and beat in egg. Season. Season lamb and spread with basil couscous. Roll up and wrap in caul fat, then roll up tightly in clingfilm. Place in fridge to set.

For the tomato confit: soak tomatoes in boiling water, skin and cut in half, remove seeds. Gently melt butter and olive oil. Add coriander seeds, chopped herbs and garlic. Place tomato halves on tray and toss with butter and oil mixture. Cook in a very low oven (100°C/lowest gas mark) for 1–2 hours until soft but still holding their shape.

For the aubergine purée: heat oven to 140°C/gas mark 1. Halve aubergines and score them on each side. Brush with olive oil, garlic slices and herbs. Wrap tightly in tinfoil, bake in oven for 1–1½ hours. Remove soft flesh, discarding skin. Purée aubergine pulp and season.

For the aubergine crisps: slice aubergine very thinly. Toss in seasoned flour and deep-fry at 170°C until crisp. Drain on absorbent paper, season and store in airtight container.

For the pesto: blend pine kernels, garlic and Parmesan with some of the olive oil until it forms a paste. Add basil leaves and the rest of the olive oil, blend until smooth and check seasoning.

For the lamb jus: heat oil in pan. Add vegetables and brown. Deglaze with port and brandy, then add chicken leg, lamb stock, chicken stock and water. Bring to the boil, skim, simmer for 1 hour and pass through muslin into clean pan. Reduce over high heat until it reaches sauce consistency.

Seal lamb in 2–3 tablespoons of hot oil (approximately 2 minutes). Cook in oven at 220°C/gas mark 7 for 5–7 minutes. Rest for 3–4 minutes. Warm sauce, tomato confit and aubergine purée.

To serve, slice each of the four pieces of lamb into 3 equal pieces and place in centre of a warmed plate. Surround with tomato confit, put a quenelle of aubergine purée on to the tomato. Top lamb with aubergine crisps and pour round sauce and pesto.

White chocolate mousse

with dark chocolate sauce

255g Valrhona Ivoire chocolate
150ml water
50g castor sugar
1¹/₂ leaves of gelatine soaked in
cold water
400ml whipped double cream
20 firm raspberries
20 small sprigs of mint
for the chocolate sauce
50g Valrhona dark chocolate (70%
cocoa solids)
125ml water
10g unsalted butter
for the dark chocolate cones
4 acetate cones
100g melted Valrhona dark
chocolate (70% cocoa solids)
for the tuille webs
50g icing sugar
50g plain flour
50g egg white
50g melted, unsalted butter

For the white chocolate mousse: place chocolate, water and sugar in a bowl and melt over hot water. Add gelatine, mix well until dissolved. Cool, making sure it doesn't set. Fold in double cream. Refrigerate until set.

For the chocolate sauce: break chocolate into very small pieces and put into a small pan with the water. Melt, then bring to the boil, whisk in butter and cool.

For the dark chocolate cones: pour melted chocolate into cones, then pour out the excess – so that the inside is thinly coated. Leave to set in a cool place (not a refrigerator).

For the tuille webs: blend icing sugar, plain flour and egg white. With blender still running pour in the butter. Place in a refrigerator to set. Best made 24 hours in advance.

Place tuille web mixture in a silicone paper piping bag and pipe web shapes on to a non-stick mat (12 large, 12 medium and 12 small. Make some extra to cover breakages as they are very fragile). Bake in an oven at 180°C/gas mark 4 until a very light golden colour, 4–6 minutes. Remove from tray and allow to go cold. Place in an airtight container until ready to use.

Pipe white chocolate mousse into dark chocolate cones, smooth off at the bottom.

Using a cocktail stick put a hole in the top of each raspberry and insert a mint sprig.

To serve, place chocolate cones in the centre of the plates. Gently put on tuille webs (largest first, then medium, then small). Place raspberries evenly around cone and pour chocolate sauce around.

Nick Nairn
Nairns and Nairns Cook School

It's been a hectic old time recently, what with setting up the cook school here at Port of Menteith, starting our outside catering business Nairns Anywhere and developing my own range of sauces with Baxter's. There's been plenty of filming too from the usual 'Ready Steady Cook', BBC 2's 'Kitchen Invaders' and a new mammoth 15 part Carlton series called 'Back to Basics'.

At the school the hard work is really starting to pay off: the day courses are really popular, and the gift vouchers have been a great success, especially with John Webber holding the classes at the school. He really is the best tutor around; patient and affable, and he takes the mystery out of cooking. Getting John on board was the best starting point for the school – his teaching skills are second to none. We also use the school as a training facility for chefs, where John teaches groups from catering giant Compass Granada – I act for them as a consultant, and they are also partners in Nairns Anywhere. My soon-to-be wife Holly is in charge of the herb and salad gardens at the school, where she grows the most fantastic range of leaves. We use these at the school and restaurant, as well as supplying a few places in Glasgow and Edinburgh.

The school is home to the main kitchens for Nairns Anywhere, our new event catering company. Our team provide the best restaurant-quality food to all sizes of events, from corporate dinners to weddings. We really do offer a truly unique experience, and it's fantastic to see the reactions when the food is served up.

All these projects are really exciting and it's great to be in a position to use past experience in such a variety of ways. It's a real privilege to work with some of the best names in the business, and reassuring that the larger companies are taking food seriously, whether that's in the staff canteen or at the director's dinner. Who knows where the next ten years will take me, although one thing is for sure: food will figure highly. At the end of the day, I love cooking and I love food and whether it's a day under pressure in the restaurant or simply unwinding by cooking dinner for friends, I'm happiest in the kitchen.

Shellfish and saffron broth

with green herb potato dumplings

for the broth

1 litre good fish stock

300ml fresh tomato sauce

4 eggs

a pinch of saffron threads

for the green paste (this makes a lot!)

90g coriander leaves, stalks and roots

40g mint leaves

8 cloves of garlic, peeled

2 tsp cumin

1 tsp sugar

1 tsp salt

75ml lime or lemon juice

5–10 green chillies, deseeded

100ml creamed coconut

for the potato dumplings

225g mashed potato

50g plain white flour

2–3 tbsp green paste (see above)

1 small lobster, cooked, meat removed and cut into chunks

12 langoustines (Dublin Bay prawns), cooked and shelled

450g fresh mussels, cooked and shelled

8 large scallops, roes removed and lightly poached

Simon Hopkinson is responsible for creating the absurdly delicious green paste used here – I always have it to hand in the fridge.

First make the broth – this involves clarifying it, but it's easier to do than you think! Put fish stock and tomato sauce into a large saucepan with crushed shells and whites of 4 eggs. Now bring slowly to the boil, whisking vigorously with a balloon whisk until a crust forms. Stop whisking just before it boils and allow crust to rise to the top of the pan. Turn off heat and let it settle for a couple of minutes, then raise heat and let crust rise again. Do this three times. Line a sieve with a bit of muslin or a J-cloth, place over a clean saucepan and pour stock through it, keeping the crust back. The stock will be crystal clear! Add saffron strands to stock and simmer for 10 minutes, then taste and season.

Meanwhile, make the green paste – just whizz it all up in the blender and spoon into a storage jar to keep in the fridge (cover with a layer of olive oil).

Next make the dumplings. Beat potato with flour and green paste until well mixed. Break off into tiny lumps and roll into balls. Place on a greased tray. Drop them into broth and poach them for a minute or two, until they float to the surface, then scoop them out and keep warm.

Next add seafood to broth for 1 minute to heat through, then return dumplings to the pan. Carefully ladle soup into warm bowls, making sure that each person gets a fair share of the seafood!

Pan-fried partridge

with Stornoway black pudding and mixed leaves

4 partridges
Maldon salt and freshly ground
black pepper
1 tbsp olive oil
150ml stock and red wine, mixed
(125ml stock, 25 wine)
1 tsp redcurrant jelly
4 thick slices best black pudding
(mine comes from Stornoway!)
250g mixed salad leaves, washed
and dried
3 tbsp vinaigrette

I've used partridge here, but we often serve this at the restaurant using mallard instead. Pigeon would also work very well. Game and black pudding work really well together, especially when contrasted with lovely fresh salad leaves grown for the restaurant by the gardener and now my fiancée, Holly!

Carefully remove breasts from birds and pull off skin (keep carcasses and legs to make stock). Season partridge breasts with salt and pepper. Heat a heavy-based frying pan until very hot. Add 1 tablespoon of oil to pan then breasts, skinned-side down. Fry for 2 minutes then turn over and fry for 2 minutes more. Remove partridge from pan and allow to rest on a plate in a warm place. Deglaze pan with stock and red wine, stir in the redcurrant jelly, reduce by half, then set aside and keep warm.

Fry black pudding in a non-stick pan until crisp on the outside and heated through. Cut or tear slices into bite-sized pieces.

To serve, slice partridge thinly. Place a mound of dressed salad leaves on 4 plates. Arrange partridge on top or around salad. Surround with chunks of black pudding and drizzle with the reduced jus. Serve immediately.

Seared monkfish on rösti

with spinach and a herb butter sauce

for the rösti potatoes

500g potatoes, such as Golden
Wonder, Maris Piper or Cyprus
Maldon salt and freshly ground
black pepper
8 tsp olive oil

450g leaf spinach, washed and
drained
1 tbsp sunflower oil
15g butter
750g monkfish fillets, trimmed of all
membrane

for the herb butter sauce

600ml vegetable or fish stock
200g chilled butter, diced
1 tsp lemon juice
Maldon salt and freshly ground
white pepper
4 tbsp fresh parsley and basil,
chopped

As with all straightforward dishes, the raw ingredients are of prime importance and this means good roasting spuds, preferably Golden Wonder, Maris Piper or other potatoes with a high potato mass (which makes them feel heavy) and a low sugar content. The monkfish should be spanking fresh, white and firm. The spinach should have thick leaves with the biggest stalks removed – tedious, I know, but worth it.

For the rösti potatoes: peel potatoes, coarsely grate them into a bowl and squeeze out as much moisture as possible. Season with a teaspoon of salt and some pepper. Heat half the oil in 4 individual 12.5cm blini pans. Add potato mix and press it down evenly with the back of a spatula. Fry over a low–medium heat for about 15 minutes until you can see traces of colour at the edges – but take care not to cook it over too high a heat or it will over-brown before potato on the inside has had a chance to cook. Cover pans with an inverted plate, hold the two together and turn over so that rösti is transferred to the plate. Heat remaining oil and butter in pan. Slide rösti back in on its uncooked side and cook for another 10–15 minutes until golden. Now you can either keep rösti warm, or leave to cool and reheat later in the oven at 180°C/gas mark 4 for 5 minutes.

For the spinach: heat sunflower oil in a large pan, add spinach and stir-fry over a high heat until it wilts into the bottom. Tip it into a colander, gently press out excess liquid and then return it to pan and toss with the butter and some seasoning. Keep it warm.

For the herb butter sauce: boil stock over a high heat until reduced to about 100ml. Turn down heat, chuck in all the butter and whisk like mad (or use a stick blender) until butter is amalgamated and sauce light and slightly thickened. Stir in lemon juice and seasoning, then parsley and basil. You can keep this warm in a Thermos!

Next, cook the monkfish. Heat a large, heavy frying pan until very hot, add a little oil and monkfish fillet. Fry over a high heat for about 4 minutes on each side until nicely brown and only just cooked through to the centre. Cut cooked monkfish into 12–16 pieces.

To serve, place individual röstis in the centres of 4 warm plates. Spoon on some of the spinach, pile a quarter of the monkfish on top of each and then spoon over butter sauce. Serve immediately.

Hot raspberry soufflés

500g fresh or frozen raspberries
190g castor sugar
a little butter for greasing
350ml milk
3 medium fresh organic egg yolks
(keep the whites)
15g cornflour
15g plain flour
6 medium fresh organic egg whites
icing sugar, to dust

(Serves 6)

The intensity of flavour in these pretty pink soufflés is amazing. You can use your best raspberry jam instead of fresh rasps – but watch the sweetness!

Press raspberries through a sieve or blitz in a food processor then sieve to remove seeds. Add 50g of the sugar and stir over a gentle heat until sugar has dissolved. Bring mixture to the boil and boil rapidly for about 10 minutes, stirring frequently towards the end of cooking, until you are left with a thick 'jam'.

Slide a baking sheet on to the middle shelf of the oven and preheat it to 200°C/gas mark 6. Lightly butter six 7.5cm ramekins and dust them out with a little extra castor sugar.

Pour all but 1 tablespoon of the milk into a pan and slowly bring it to the boil. Meanwhile, beat egg yolks, another 40g castor sugar, cornflour, plain flour and remaining milk together in a bowl until smooth. Whisk in hot milk, return mixture to pan and bring to the boil, stirring. Reduce heat and leave mixture to simmer very gently for about 10 minutes, beating it every now and then, until you have cooked out the taste of the flour.

Pour custard into a bowl and beat in the raspberry 'jam'. Whisk egg whites into soft peaks and then whisk in the remaining castor sugar. Lightly whisk one-quarter of the whites into custard to loosen it slightly, then carefully fold in the remainder. Spoon mixture into prepared ramekins, level tops and then run the tip of a knife around the inside edge of each dish to release the mixture. Slide the ramekins on to baking sheet and bake for 10–12 minutes until soufflés are well risen, browned and doubled in height but still slightly wobbly.

Quickly lift them on to small dessert plates, sprinkle with a little more castor (or icing) sugar and serve straight away, before they've had time to sink!

Ferrier Richardson and Steven Caputa
Eurasia

At Eurasia we use the best Scottish produce seasoned with Asian herbs and spices to create a modern cuisine that's all about taste. I've always been heavily influenced by the east, not just the food, but also style and philosophy – the way everything is ordered and organised – and a belief in the importance of the family. The great thing about Asian cuisine is that all the elements in a dish are there for a reason – there's nothing just for show. At Eurasia we can follow all these principles, at the same time as being able to benefit from the outstanding quality and abundance of Scotland's natural produce. So much has happened to Scottish cooking over the last ten years. It's like the Scots have realised they can cook! Everyone says it now, but it's so true: Scotland has an unbeatable natural larder, and it's very encouraging to see how much more our local produce is used these days.

I'm active in the 'Culinary Excellence Programme' which involves school children in the catering industry. I'm very conscious of the fact that the industry's not perfect, but there are so many opportunities for young people and not just in the kitchen – that's one of the messages I'm keen to get across. There's front-of-house work, but also a whole range of other careers: lawyers, journalists, designers, photographers – you name it, it can be done in the catering business! And in Scotland, traditional trades such as engineering and shipbuilding no longer employ the huge number of people they used to, so learning the kinds of transferable skills you need in a restaurant or hotel is a sensible thing to do. If you can cope with the hours and the demands of the customers, you can cope with anything! I've been working with the students for five years now and I really enjoy it. I love seeing the way their confidence grows. It's also very cheering to find that 60% of the children involved in the 'Culinary Excellence Programme' go on to further training or straight into work in the catering industry – at the start, we had estimated it would be around 10%. Off the back of this scheme, we have now created our own school where we induct six full-time students every six months. All in all I think we have a bright future ahead.

Carpaccio
of Aberdeen Angus

with a Parmesan tuille and daikon salad

350g fillet of beef
250g Reggiano Parmesan, grated
50g mixed leaves
15ml vegetable oil
10ml sesame oil
salt and pepper
200g daikon (Japanese radish), shredded
15ml coriander oil
15ml chilli sauce

Slice raw beef wafer thin.

Prepare tuille baskets by sprinkling grated Parmesan in a rectangle on a non-stick baking sheet. Cook in an oven at 180°C/gas mark 4 until a light golden brown. Allow to cool slightly then roll round rolling pin to create a tube to hold salad.

Dress mixed leaves with vegetable and sesame oil, season and place in bottom of Parmesan tuille and top with shredded daikon.

Place beef on a plate, add Parmesan tuille and salad, dress with coriander oil and chilli sauce (both of which can be bought in any good Asian supermarket).

Roast supreme of cod

with bok choi, spring onions, ginger and

basil butter sauce

4 x 175g cod fillets (skin on)
3 tbsp vegetable oil
4 large baking potatoes, cooked
1 large egg
salt and pepper
8 pieces of bok choi
32 spring onions
50ml fish stock
1 tbsp finely grated ginger
150ml double cream
60g butter
44 large basil leaves

Pan-fry cod in hot frying pan with vegetable oil. Transfer to heatproof dish and cook for 17 minutes at 200°C/gas mark 6.

Grate potato, mix with egg and season and create 4 potato cakes. Pan fry until golden brown.

Steam bok choi and spring onion till tender.

Add ginger to fish stock and reduce by half, add double cream and reduce till sauce coats back of spoon. Pass through fine strainer. Finish with butter and 20 leaves of shredded basil.

Deep-fry 24 basil leaves until crispy (in a deep fat fryer).

Place potato cake on plate, top with bok choi then the cod. Place spring onions to form a square then fill centre with sauce. Top with 6 fried basil leaves.

Lightly curried leek and potato soup

with a smoked haddock spring roll

60g butter
180g potato, diced
180g leeks, sliced
90g onions, sliced
60g curry powder
salt and pepper
500ml vegetable stock
30g coriander leaves
125ml double cream
for the spring roll
120g smoked haddock
60g spring onions
30g garlic, finely diced
30g red chilli, finely diced
30g butter
30g coriander
30g sweet chilli sauce
4 spring roll sheets

Melt butter in a heavy-based pan. Add potato dice, sliced leeks, onion, curry powder and seasoning. Cook for approximately 5 minutes over a medium heat – do not allow to colour.

Add vegetable stock, bring to the boil and then simmer until vegetables are cooked. Add coriander. Remove from heat and liquidise.

Return to pan and finish with cream. Do not boil.

For the spring roll: sauté together smoked haddock, spring onion, garlic and chilli with butter until lightly cooked.

Remove from pan and cool, then add coriander and sweet chilli sauce (this sauce is available from any good Asian supermarket).

Brush spring roll sheets with water, then place haddock mixture on and roll.

Deep-fry at 180°C/gas mark 4 (in a deep fat fryer).

Serve soup in a warm bowl and place spring roll on a Chinese spoon beside the soup bowl.

Chocolate soufflé

with vanilla ice cream

for the soufflé base

500ml milk

110g sugar

1 vanilla pod, split

40g flour

50g cocoa powder

6 egg yolks

for the tuille mix

225g diced butter

225g icing sugar

1 tbsp vanilla essence

240 ml egg white

225g flour

for the vanilla ice cream

6 egg yolks

120g sugar

500ml milk

2 vanilla pods, split

for the soufflé

225g egg whites

150g sugar

300g soufflé base

50g butter

For the soufflé base: in a heavy-based pot add milk, sugar and vanilla pod, bring to the boil. Leave to infuse for 5 minutes.

In a mixing bowl add flour, cocoa powder and egg yolks beaten until smooth. Pour over half the milk mixture, while whisking, then return to the pan. Return to heat and bring back to the boil. Cool and reserve.

For the tuille: cream the butter and sugar together until white, add vanilla essence and egg whites and pulse until well incorporated. Sieve in the flour. Refrigerate until needed.

For the vanilla ice cream: whisk the yolks and sugar to reach a sabayon (i.e. white and doubled in volume).

In a heavy-based pot bring milk and vanilla pods to the boil. Leave to infuse for 5 minutes. Pour half the milk over the sabayon while whisking. Return to the pot and return to the heat and bring gently to the boil, stirring constantly, until it coats the back of the spoon.

Chill and freeze.

For the soufflé: whip the egg whites until soft peak stage, add 110g sugar (to form Italian meringue). Fold gently into the soufflé base.

Grease a ramekin or ovenware dish with butter then line with remaining sugar. Bake at 190°C/gas mark 5 for 8 minutes.

Shirley Spear
The Three Chimneys

We came to the Three Chimneys over sixteen years ago, when the children were only five and three. I'm from the Borders and always knew I wanted to come back to Scotland. I'd been working in public relations for British Gas and a high point of my job was taking journalists to lunch in good London restaurants. That was in the late 1970s, when British cooking was really taking off. It was a wonderful time to be in London, but it's been even better to have been part of the burgeoning Scottish restaurant scene through the 80s and 90s.

When I worked in London, I did used to get very cross when people made negative comments about Scottish cooking. I knew that the Scots had the best natural produce to hand, and were great at baking and cooking, but that this was a strongly home-based tradition. I'd been brought up in this, and loved to cook.

I met Eddie – he was my driving instructor – and we were supposed to go out for dinner on our first date, but in the end I cooked for him and he loved it! That was the start of what I call our "dinner-table dreams" – to come to Scotland and try our hand at running a restaurant. We weren't very ambitious, we just wanted to try a different way of living – away from Croydon, and commuting. We never imagined we'd be so successful or really how hard we'd have to work.

My first night was terrifying, and chaotic. I had to teach myself all the techniques of restaurant cooking very quickly. I still cook some basic, everyday Scottish food, but my food has refined and developed over the years – I've learned from the fantastic local produce we have here on Skye, learned to make the most of it. Flavour is all important, and it must reflect the reality of the contents of the dish.

We have wonderful suppliers, including a local market gardener who keeps us stocked with tasty and beautiful salad leaves and herbs. We like to keep things local whenever we can. In 1999, we built six rooms next to the restaurant, called the House Over-By. We used a local architect, builder and interior designer. A local graphic designer created our new logo and brochure.

Three Chimneys
Skye crab tian

for the base

2 tbsp good olive oil

the white and pale green of 2 large spring onions, very finely chopped

1 medium red chilli, deseeded and very finely chopped

1 clove of garlic, crushed

200g arborio rice

450ml hot crab stock (make up to 750ml with a mixture of wine and water – liquid must be piping hot when poured into rice)

125g white crabmeat

sea salt and white pepper

2–3 tsp lemon juice

2 tbsp freshly grated Parmesan

2 tbsp fresh coriander, finely chopped

rind of 1 lime

for the topping

125g white crab meat

125g brown crab meat

juice of 2 limes

sea salt and white pepper

for the dressing

125g brown crab meat

125g thick, Greek-style yoghurt

2 tsp good quality tomato passata

sea salt and white pepper

2 tsp lemon juice

fresh coriander leaves, to garnish

salad leaves, to garnish

For the base: line a cake tin, approximately 20cm square and 5cm deep, with baking parchment paper. Heat olive oil in a large saucepan or, preferably, a wide, deep frying pan. Stir spring onion, lime rind, chilli and garlic in the hot oil for a few seconds. Add rice and stir well to coat with oil. Pour in half the hot stock mixture and stir well. Allow rice to absorb the liquid. This will take approximately 10 minutes. Keep adding stock until rice is cooked al dente, fluffy in appearance and no longer absorbing liquid easily. Add white crab meat to rice and thoroughly heat through. Check for seasoning and add lemon juice to taste. Remove from heat. Stir in Parmesan cheese and fresh coriander. Pack the risotto mixture into the lined cake tin evenly. Leave to chill in the refrigerator, preferably overnight. Cut round shapes with a 5cm round cutter before serving.

Leftover base mix can be reshaped into a block, wrapped and frozen for a later date, when further round shapes can be cut out. The rice mixture also makes great canapés.

For the topping: mix all ingredients together, cover and refrigerate before use.

For the dressing: put crabmeat, yoghurt and tomato passata in blender and liquidise until smooth. Season with salt and pepper and add lemon juice to taste.

To serve, drizzle dressing over the plate. Place crab risotto shape on top. Pile mixture of crab meat on top of risotto. Garnish with fresh coriander and salad leaves dressed with lemon juice and olive oil.

Grilled loin of lamb

with leek and mushroom pearl barley risotto and wild garlic gravy

1 x ½ loin of lamb
200g assorted wild mushrooms
50g butter
4 tbsp double cream
for the marinade
8 tbsp olive oil
2 strips of orange peel (no pith)
2 sprigs of rosemary
2 cloves of garlic, crushed with the flat blade of the knife
8 black peppercorns, lightly crushed
a pinch of rock salt
for the pearl barley
2 tbsp olive oil
1 medium leek (avoid too much dark green), chopped finely
1 medium onion, chopped finely
200g pearl barley, rinsed in cold water and drained through a sieve
50g plump raisins
50g pine nuts
finely grated rind of ½ orange
1 tsp fresh rosemary, finely chopped
salt and pepper, freshly ground
600ml lamb or light vegetable stock
300ml good quality red wine

You will need 1 whole half loin of lamb for 4 people. Ask the butcher to strip the loin from the bone and trim it down to the 'eye'. Remove the fat. Keep the bones to make a good lamb stock for the wild garlic gravy, or any other sauce that you decide to serve. The stock can also be used to make the pearl barley risotto (see below).

Marinade the strip loin of lamb for up to 4 hours before cooking. Pour marinade ingredients over meat in a suitable flat dish, cover and refrigerate before cooking.

For the pearl barley: heat oil in a wide, heavy-based pan. Stir finely-chopped leek and onion in hot oil until beginning to soften. Add pearl barley and keep turning it in hot oil until it starts to colour pale brown. Add raisins, pine nuts, orange rind, rosemary and seasoning. Stir all together well. Pour in stock and wine. Bring to the boil and simmer uncovered until all the liquid has been absorbed. The pearl barley should be cooked al dente. This mixture can be cooled and stored in a refrigerator at this stage.

For the wild garlic gravy: wild garlic is only available in late spring, therefore this recipe can only be made at that time of year. However you can follow the basic principle and flavour the sauce with different herbs, such as rosemary and thyme, and jellies, such as rowan or redcurrant, and red wine or port instead of Madeira. Pick wild garlic leaves as fresh as possible before using. The pretty white flowers are edible and can be used to garnish the dish.

Melt butter in a wide, heavy-based pan. Soften onion in hot butter. Add crushed garlic clove and mushrooms, plus half the wild garlic and seasonings. Stir together well and allow to cook for a minute or two. Add the Madeira. Bring to the boil and reduce liquid until it has virtually all been absorbed and mixture is thick and syrupy. Add lamb stock, bring back to the boil and reduce again by half. Strain sauce through a fine sieve. Press all the liquid through. You should be left with 250ml for the gravy.

for the wild garlic gravy

50g unsalted butter

1 medium onion, finely chopped

125g mushrooms, chopped small (use up trimmings, stalks etc for the prepared risotto)

2 large handfuls of wild garlic leaves, washed and roughly chopped

ground rock salt and black pepper

1 bay leaf

125ml Madeira

500ml well-flavoured lamb stock

1 fat clove of garlic, crushed with the flat blade of a knife

1 tsp arrowroot

To finish, dissolve 1 level teaspoon of arrowroot in 1 tablespoon of the liquid. Mix until smooth. Add this to gravy in a small saucepan and return to the heat. Bring to the boil, stirring all the time until mixture is very lightly thickened. Last of all, throw in another handful of finely chopped garlic leaves. Leave these to infuse in sauce for extra flavour. Reheat and strain gravy before pouring over the cooked meat.

To finish, grill the whole piece of lamb under a high heat for approximately 3–5 minutes on each side and then leave to rest in a warm place before cutting into 4 portions and slicing. This cut of lamb is very tender and only needs to be cooked lightly. It should be pink in the middle.

Roughly chop wild mushrooms, or whatever you can obtain, depending on the time of year. Melt butter in a medium/large sauté pan and turn mushrooms in hot butter. Add 2 tablespoons of pearl barley mixture per person to the pan. Stir together well. Add cream; stir well until all is heated thoroughly. Spoon on to plate as a bed for the meat, or shape in a vegetable ring mould as illustrated. Finally, pile a few more sautéed mushrooms on top of risotto.

Along with the pearl barley risotto, we serve the lamb on a bed of spinach, 'wilted' quickly in hot butter with freshly ground black pepper and freshly grated nutmeg immediately before serving. Pour the sauce around the meat.

Grilled lobster vanille

2 firm, lively lobsters,
approx $^1/_2$ kilo in weight each
4-6 langoustine tails per person,
cooked and shelled
4 heaped tbsp fine white
breadcrumbs
2 tbsp good quality Parmesan
50g unsalted butter
a squeeze of lemon juice
rock salt and ground white pepper
4 tsps double cream
for the vanilla sauce
1 vanilla pod
250ml good fish stock
2 tbsp dry vermouth
250ml double cream
125ml milk
6 egg yolks
1 tbsp lemon juice

Plunge lobsters into a deep pan of well-salted, fast-boiling water and cover saucepan with a lid. Retain a high heat under saucepan and by the time water has come back to the boil the lobsters will be lightly cooked and the colour of their shells will have transformed from dark blue to bright red. Remove lobsters from boiling water and plunge them into a bowl of ice-cold water to cool them down as quickly as possible. This arrests further cooking within the heat of their own shells.

When lobsters are cold, remove claws and cut each lobster in half, straight down the middle. Remove stomach sac at the head end and the intestinal track that runs the length of the tail. Discard these. Crack claws with a sharp tap from a small hammer or a heavy, blunt instrument such as the end of a rolling pin. Remove claw meat carefully and try to retain shape of claws as perfectly as possible. Remove meat from the tail in one whole piece and cut into 4 chunks. If you have a lobster with red roes inside it or greeny black tomalley, remove this also and stir into sauce for added flavour and great colour.

Set aside meat from each half lobster and add 4–6 langoustine tails, removed from the shell, to each portion. Keep lobster shell intact, head and tail still joined together with legs and long red feeler.

For the vanilla sauce: take vanilla pod, cut it in half lengthwise and scrape out seeds, which will resemble a black paste. Keep seeds on one side and place pod in a saucepan with fish stock, plus dry vermouth. Bring this to the boil and reduce by half to 125ml.

Remove pod and add double cream and milk to saucepan. Return to the heat and warm until it is just beginning to bubble around the edges.

Meanwhile, whisk egg yolks together with lemon juice in a bowl. Pour over warm milk and cream mixture, whisking all the time. Return this mixture to saucepan and heat it slowly until it thickens like a custard. Stir all the time and watch it carefully. When sauce is thick enough to coat the back of a wooden spoon, pour it immediately into a clean bowl or jug, and stand it in a bowl of iced water to cool down quickly. This will help to prevent sauce from scrambling as it continues to cook in its own heat. Stir in vanilla seeds. Leave to cool completely. Sauce can be stored for later use in the refrigerator.

To finish, mix together the breadcrumbs with Parmesan cheese.

Melt butter in a wide saucepan together with a few drops of fresh lemon juice, a twist of rock salt and white pepper. Put prepared lobster and langoustines into pan and gently turn and coat in butter. It is easier to do this in two separate lots than all 4 portions at once. For 2 portions, add 4 tablespoons of sauce to the lobster together with two teaspoons of cream. Fold lobster and langoustines very gently together with sauce and warm through carefully.

Place half the lobster shells on a baking sheet lined with foil. Pile lobster and langoustines, with sauce, back into empty lobster shells. Use any remaining sauce in the pan to cover meat liberally, filling in all the gaps. Sprinkle the top with breadcrumbs. Place tray of lobster in the bottom of the grill to keep warm, while you prepare the second tray of lobster, using more sauce and the last two teaspoons of cream.

When all the lobster is ready, place both trays directly under a very hot grill to give dish a final blast of heat, while browning the breadcrumbs on top. The mixture should show signs of sizzling and bubbling up around the edges.

Transfer the whole hot lobster to a hot dish and serve immediately. We accompany this dish with a timbale of basmati rice flavoured with lemon, cardamom and fresh herbs, together with dressed salad leaves.

Iced damson parfait

750g damsons
1 level tbsp castor sugar
150ml water
125g granulated sugar
3 large eggs
150ml double cream
ripe pears, to garnish

(Serves 8)

Line a terrine-shaped loaf tin or an ordinary 900g loaf tin with clingfilm, making sure the clingfilm overlaps the rim of the tin generously.

To prepare fruit: wash damsons. Keep whole and place in a saucepan with 2 tablespoons of water. Cover with a lid and cook over a low heat until fruit is soft and pulpy. Strain cooked fruit through a fine mesh sieve and reserve juice. Press fruit through sieve into a bowl. You should be left with a thick fruit purée in the bowl and skins and stones from the damsons in the sieve. Press as much of the fruit pulp through sieve as you can. Measure damson purée in a measuring jug. You should have a yield of approximately 450ml of purée from the original amount of fruit.

While purée is still hot, stir in castor sugar to sweeten to taste. Do not overdo the sugar at this stage, as sharpness of fruit will be reduced again with the addition of other ingredients. Set purée aside.

To make damson syrup: reheat damson juice in a saucepan. Stir in enough castor sugar to sweeten juice to your taste. Dissolve sugar thoroughly then boil rapidly for about 5 minutes until liquid reduces a little and becomes syrupy. Pour into a suitable container, cool and keep chilled in the refrigerator until required.

To make parfait: put water and granulated sugar into a saucepan. Stir over a low heat until all the sugar is dissolved. Then bring to the boil and bubble fiercely for 3 minutes, to make a sugar syrup. Fit a heat-resistant pudding basin over a pan of simmering water, making sure that it fits snugly and that the bottom of the bowl is not touching the water. Whisk eggs in bowl until frothy, then pour on boiling sugar syrup. This must be done with care. Do not let hot syrup touch the cool whisk as this may set the syrup. Continue to whisk egg and syrup mixture over simmering water until mixture is pale and mousse-like. The whisk will leave a ribbon trail in mixture when lifted out. Next, lift the basin off the pan of water (take care that steam doesn't scald you) and whisk again until mixture is cooled down. This can be done with bowl standing in a basin of iced water to speed things up. Whip double cream until it holds its shape but is not solid. Fold cream and damson purée together thoroughly. Fold mixture into egg mixture. Do not over-stir or you will knock out all the air. Pour finished mixture into loaf tin and freeze.

To serve, unmould frozen parfait on to a flat serving dish. Peel off clingfilm. Using a knife dipped in hot water, slice parfait and place on individual plates for serving. Pour damson syrup around and garnish with thin slices of ripe pear. There will be enough parfait for at least 8 people. What you do not want can be wrapped and kept frozen for another occasion.

Mike Stoddart and Eddie McDonald
The Marcliffe at Pitfodels

Mike: Stewart Spence took over the original Marcliffe – a hotel in Aberdeen's old town, owned by a couple called Marion and Clifford – and then opened the New Marcliffe, before building this hotel at Pitfodels in 1993. I've worked for Stewart on and off for fourteen years; he's a great boss, and I can't really imagine working for anyone else – except myself, one day.

I was a baker for a year before I became a chef. My gran was very good at baking, and my parents worked in the hotel and catering industry, front of house. I started cooking for them on Saturday nights when I was quite young, and that's how I got interested in being a chef. I'm a very hands-on Executive Chef at the Marcliffe. The hardest thing about my job is getting staff, and staff who have been trained. Stewart Spence is heavily involved in Hospitality Training. Bad-tempered celebrity chefs haven't helped the profession much in recent years – I'm not into shouting at staff. This is a busy hotel, the only Scottish Tourist Board 5 star hotel in the north of Scotland. We get lots of weddings and banqueting, as well as locals from Aberdeen. My philosophy of cooking is simple food, cooked properly. I'm also a great believer in the use of salt and pepper – I think a lot of chefs don't know how to do that anymore.

Eddie: I count myself rather fortunate in the start I received in the hospitality industry. Being undecided on my career path, I was certainly open to suggestions. Just at the right time, a family friend informed me of a job opening at the Waterside Hotel, Peterhead – this opportunity really helped me in my decision to become a chef. It was a fantastic place and I learnt a tremendous amount from Tony Jackson (Scottish Culinary Team Manager), Robert Bruce and Graham Buchan (both members of the Scottish Culinary Team), to name but a few talents. From such a group of professionals, I gained the motivation, discipline and high standards I was striving for, and which I hold by today. There is a buzz in a busy kitchen that really drives me. I love the creativity involved, and the satisfaction of seeing a happy customer. With high quality, fresh produce, handled, cooked and presented well without too much fuss, you can't go far wrong. It helps if it tastes great too!

Mike Stoddart and Eddie McDonald
The Marcliffe at Pitfodels

Pan-seared scallops

with a pepper, corn and avocado salsa and spiced tuille

for the tuille
110g butter
12g icing sugar
1–2 egg whites
110g flour, sieved
cracked black pepper

for the salsa
juice and zest of 1 lemon
juice of ½ lime
50ml olive oil
2 tsp sweet chilli sauce
1 yellow pepper
1 red pepper
2 plum tomatoes
2 spring onions
6 pieces of baby corn
1 avocado, peeled
pinch of coriander leaves
½ red onion, finely sliced
olive oil
12 scallops
knob of butter
salt and pepper
4 sprigs of coriander

For the tuille: preheat oven to190°C/gas mark 5. In a bowl, cream butter and sugar, gradually beat in egg whites, then fold in flour until you have a smooth paste. Chill for at least 2 hours.

Spread on to a non-stick baking sheet, using a template of your chosen shape and mill on some black pepper and bake for about 4 minutes until mixture is just beginning to colour. Remove from oven and leave to cool.

For the salsa: remove zest from lemon and blanch in boiling water until soft; drain and place in bowl.

Squeeze the juice of lemon and lime into bowl, add olive oil and chilli sauce.

Remove skin from peppers and tomato, deseed and cut into even dice. Wash spring onion and slice finely.

Slice corn and quickly fry in a little olive oil. Scoop or cut avocado into small pieces. Add everything to bowl and mix all the ingredients gently to coat with juices; season as required.

Heat a frying pan until very hot then add a thin film of olive oil. Place scallops into hot pan, cooking for about 1 minute on each side. When you turn the scallops add a knob of butter to help them colour. Season to taste once they are almost cooked.

To serve, spoon a little salsa in the centre of the plate and place 3 lightly cooked scallops around it. Place peppered tuille on scallops; add a small amount of salsa on tuille and garnish with a sprig of fresh coriander.

Roasted venison striploin

with walnut and potato purée and beetroot confit

for the sauce

1 onion

1 carrot

1 leek

1 stalk of celery

$^1/_2$ head of garlic

olive oil

$^1/_2$ bottle red wine

1 sprig of thyme

1 tbsp redcurrant jelly

5 litres brown stock (veal or beef)

butter

for the venison

4 x 200g venison striploin

8 rashers of streaky bacon

salt and pepper

olive oil

redcurrants, to garnish

brambles, to garnish

for the confit

4 beetroot, approximately 800g total

100ml duck fat

1 tbsp red wine vinegar

1 tbsp balsamic vinegar

2 sprigs of thyme

200ml water

100ml olive oil

for the walnut and potato purée

500g potatoes

25g butter

nutmeg

salt and pepper

50g walnuts

175g breadcrumbs

for choux paste

$^1/_4$ litre water

3g salt

95g butter

125g flour

4 medium eggs

for the egg wash

3 medium eggs

275ml milk

For the sauce: chop vegetables roughly. Heat a heavy-bottomed pan with a little oil, add vegetables and allow to colour. Pour on red wine, add jelly and reduce by half. Add stock, bring to the boil, skim and reduce by two-thirds; strain through a fine sieve. Finish by working in a few knobs of cold butter and chopped fresh thyme.

Wrap each piece of venison with 2 rashers of bacon (trim off any excess). Then roll them tightly in clingfilm to give a good shape. Leave for 2 hours then unwrap. Season venison with salt and pepper. Heat a heavy-based pan until very hot, add oil and then venison and colour well, frying for 4–5 minutes approximately (it may require more). Cover pan with foil, keep warm and allow meat to rest.

For the confit: wash beetroot well but do not peel. Cook beetroot in plenty of salted boiling water until tender, approximately 1 hour depending on size. Once cooked, peel and cut into wedges. To finish confit, heat the duck fat in a large pan, add beetroot wedges, red wine vinegar, balsamic vinegar and sprigs of fresh thyme, and roast in an oven preheated to 180°C/gas mark 4 for about 15 minutes. Then place pan on a high heat, add water, bring to the boil, add olive oil. Remove from heat and season. Keep warm.

For the walnut and potato purée: peel and rinse potatoes, place in a saucepan of salted water and bring to the boil. Remove any scum from the top of the water. Lower heat so that water is not boiling too rapidly, cook until soft, drain well. Then return to pan and dry out on a low heat. When dry pass through a sieve then mix in butter, nutmeg and season to taste. Roast walnuts at 180°C/gas mark 4 for 2-3 minutes. Remove walnut skins by rubbing in a cloth, then crush. Add to the breadcrumbs. Place water, salt and butter in a pan and bring to the boil. Remove from heat, add flour and mix it in with a wooden spoon. Place back on stove and continue to mix until the paste leaves the spoon clean. Remove from heat and mix in eggs one at a time, mixing each egg well in before adding the next. Mix potato with 150g choux paste, divide into approximately 50g pieces, mould with a spoon and oiled hand. Dip in egg wash and roll in breadcrumb mix, then deep-fry in very hot fat for approximately 5 minutes.

To serve, spoon beetroot confit on to a warm plate, carve 2 or 3 pieces of venison and lay on to confit, add fried potatoes and spoon on jus. Garnish with some warm redcurrants and brambles.

Beef fillet

with roasted garlic butter, wild mushrooms, baby spinach
and fine pasta

2 cloves of garlic
200g butter
bunch of parsley, chopped
olive oil
4 x 200g beef fillet
250g mixed wild mushrooms
1 tbsp cep oil
salt and pepper
300g linguine pasta
500g spinach leaves, picked
400ml cream
100ml beef jus

Roast garlic in a hot oven until it has softened slightly; remove and allow to cool. Pop it out of its skin and crush with a heavy knife. Blend with butter and half of chopped parsley, roll into a sausage shape in greaseproof paper and chill.

Heat an ovenproof pan until very hot, then add some olive oil and get this very hot. Place beef in pan and brown on all sides to seal, then add a knob of butter and place pan in a preheated oven (250°C/gas mark 9) for 6–8 minutes. Remove pan from oven and leave to rest for 2–3 minutes.

While meat is cooking sauté wild mushrooms in cep oil, season and keep warm. Cook pasta in plenty of boiling salted water, drain and keep warm. Sauté spinach in a little butter and season this at the last minute, just before plating.

To serve, place the rested beef on to a warm plate, top with a disc of garlic butter then a spoonful of wild mushrooms. Twist pasta and spinach together with a fork and set on the plate alongside beef. Deglaze hot beef pan with cream, add any jus from mushrooms, plus beef jus, bring to the boil, pass through a fine sieve, add remaining chopped parsley and spoon on to plate.

Mike Stoddart and Eddie McDonald
The Marcliffe at Pitfodels

Hot chocolate soufflé

with marshmallow ice cream and candied kumquats

for the ice cream
330ml full fat milk
4 vanilla pods
85g castor sugar
6 egg yolks
100ml whipping cream
50g white chocolate, grated

for the marshmallow
240g castor sugar
240g glucose
90ml water
2 leaves of gelatine
175ml water
1/2 tsp vanilla essence
2 egg whites

for the kumquats
20 kumquats
100g sugar
200ml water

for the soufflé
160g chocolate
6 egg whites
40g castor sugar
3 egg yolks
icing sugar, to dust
25g butter

For the ice cream: put milk and vanilla pods into a pan and bring to the boil slowly. While this is heating, whisk sugar and yolks together in a stainless-steel bowl until almost white. As soon as milk boils, whisk on to yolks. Place bowl over a pan of boiling water and stir constantly with a wooden spoon until mix starts to thicken up and coat the back of the spoon. Remove from heat straight away and pass through a fine sieve, pour into ice-cream maker and churn until almost frozen. Add whipping cream and grated white chocolate. Remove into clean container and place in deep freeze.

For the marshmallow: boil sugar, glucose and 90ml water until it reaches 127°C. Meanwhile dissolve gelatine into 175ml water. Add vanilla essence. Whisk egg whites. When in peaks pour on boiling sugar slowly. Add gelatine solution, whisk until thick, this may take a little time so use a mixer. Then spread on to greaseproof paper dusted with cornflour and freeze.

For the kumquats: blanch kumquats 4 times to remove the bitterness then add sugar and water and reduce to a syrup.

For the soufflé: melt chocolate in a bowl over a pan of boiling water. Whisk egg whites until they form peaks, adding sugar a little at a time. Fold in egg yolks. Combine with chocolate, pour into mould that has been buttered and coated with sugar. Cook in a bain-marie for 20 minutes at 190°C/gas mark 5.

To serve, spoon on the kumquats. Add ice-cream with a piece of marshmallow on it and blow-torch to glaze. De-mould soufflé, dust with icing sugar and place on plate.

David Wilson
The Peat Inn

I have always been interested in food but, in the early days, it was eating rather than cooking that I liked best. I studied marketing at Glasgow College and worked for the next twelve years in sales and marketing. I was working for an industrial engineering company in South Yorkshire, and my wife Patricia and I had just had our first child, when I decided to change direction and become a chef. We knew we wanted to run a restaurant one day and it was a case of now or never. The difficult bit was finding a place that would take me on. After a long search, I got a job working for a man called Somerset Moore who ran a country pub type restaurant serving good food. I worked away from home and travelled back only on my days off. It was a very hard year particularly the first three months when I was pretty useless at everything in the kitchen. I was used to being a middle manager and here I was chopping vegetables and taking orders from talented seventeen year-old chefs!

In 1972, we decided to settle back in Scotland and look for a restaurant of our own. We knew we didn't want to be in the city, but we couldn't afford any of the places just outside the main cities. In the end, we couldn't resist the many attractions of the Peat Inn, including the fact that it was relatively cheap (because it needed a lot done), and the unbeatable address: "The Peat Inn, Peat Inn, Fife".

When we started out, we served food in the front bar as well as in the restaurant. It was in the days when no one did bar food (except for the odd meat pie), and it was a great success, especially with the St. Andrews students. In 1979 we stopped the bar food to concentrate on the restaurant.

French cooking has always been a big influence on me, particularly a chef called Michel Guerard, from Southwest France. When we went to France on holiday, I would spend time in kitchens, watching and learning, honing my skills. To me, cooking is all about capturing the natural flavour of the food, not smothering it – clean, tasty, fresh food that looks great.

David Wilson
The Peat Inn

Dressed Anstruther crab
with yoghurt and lime and herb vinaigrette

400g white crab meat
2 heaped tbsp natural Greek yoghurt
juice of ½ lime
2 level tbsp fresh coriander leaves, chopped
50g mixed salad leaves (we suggest rocket, red chard and baby spinach)
2 large tomatoes

for the herb vinaigrette
50g fresh herbs: flat-leaf parsley, coriander, chervil – picked leaves only
50ml virgin olive oil
½ tbsp white wine vinegar
1 level tbsp lemon juice
salt and pepper

for the tomato vinaigrette
1 tomato
3 tbsp vegetable oil
2 tbsp white wine vinegar
salt and pepper

for the garnish
1 tomato, sliced thinly

If crab meat has to be removed from claws ensure no pieces of shell or 'bone' are allowed to find their way into the meat.

Spoon yoghurt on to crab meat, mix thoroughly then add lime juice and mix again. If not using immediately, cover bowl with clingfilm and refrigerate.

Just before serving, add freshly chopped coriander leaves and mix through crab.

For the herb vinaigrette: put all ingredients (except salt and pepper) in blender, blend until mix is smooth 'sauce' consistency. Check seasoning and adjust to taste.

For the tomato vinaigrette: place all ingredients in liquidiser and process until smooth. Strain through fine sieve into small bowl. Refrigerate until ready to serve.

For the garnish: place tomato slices on a Silpat mat on a baking sheet. Place on middle shelf of preheated oven (110°C) for about 2 hours, until dried. Remove, place on wire rack until cool. Store in airtight container if not using immediately.

To serve, place washed salad leaves on centre of plate.

Place ring on top (approximately 70mm x 45mm deep) fill about a third up with dressed crab. Then place slice of tomato on top, spoon in more crab, another slice of raw tomato, then more crab on top of ring. Remove ring mould.

Place thin slices of oven-dried tomato on top, drizzle herb vinaigrette around and over leaves.

Decorate with dots of tomato vinaigrette.

David Wilson
The Peat Inn

Fillet of halibut

on vegetable risotto with prawns and yellow

pepper sauce

1 tbsp olive oil
4 x 125g halibut fillets, skin
removed
12 prawns, shelled
for the vegetable risotto
1 level tbsp carrot, finely diced
1 level tbsp courgette, finely diced
1 level tbsp fennel, finely diced
1 level tbsp celery, finely diced
1 level tbsp red onion, finely diced
700ml fish stock
300g risotto rice
25g freshly grated Parmesan
15g unsalted butter
salt and pepper
for the yellow pepper sauce
1 yellow pepper
200ml vegetable stock
2 level tsp double cream
15g unsalted butter, diced
salt and pepper
for the tuille
1 egg white
20g sifted plain flour
20g melted butter
$1/3$ level tbsp fresh fennel, chopped
squeeze of lemon juice
rind of slice of lemon, grated

Put olive oil in a heavy pan over heat. When beginning to smoke, place halibut portions in pan presentation side down. Cook for 3–4 minutes to get nice colour, turn over and cook for a further minute on other side. Repeat for each fillet. Place on warm tray and hold in cool oven or hotplate until required.

For the risotto: blanch vegetables in boiling, salted water for 2 minutes. Put fish stock in pan and bring to the boil. Put risotto rice in second pan over heat, add a little of the fish stock. Stir until absorbed, then keep adding stock and stirring until all is absorbed. Rice should be cooked and glutinous. Stir in grated Parmesan and butter – this will enrich sauce and add 'shine'. Add blanched vegetables, then check seasoning. Keep warm.

For the yellow pepper sauce: roast yellow pepper under grill and remove skin. Chop into small pieces. Place pepper and vegetable stock in liquidiser and process until pepper is completely liquidised. Put in a pan, bring to a simmer, add double cream, then whisk in unsalted butter, until all is incorporated into sauce. Check seasoning, adjust to taste.

Put a film of oil in sauté pan over heat. When smoking, place prawns in pan, cook for 1 minute then turn and cook for another 1 minute. Remove from heat and keep warm.

For the tuille: whisk egg white until frothy. Fold in sifted flour. Add melted butter, fennel, lemon juice and zest. Mix together. Spoon mixture on to Silpat mat, spread with back of spoon to shape approximately 8cm x 2cm, to yield at least 4 tuilles.

To serve, place ring mould (approximately 85mm diameter x 30mm deep) on centre of plate. Spoon in risotto until level with top. Place cooked halibut on top. Place 3 small spoonfuls of risotto on plate around side, then put cooked prawns on top of risotto. Spoon yellow pepper sauce around fish. Decorate top of halibut with herb and lemon tuille.

David Wilson
The Peat Inn

Medallions of venison saddle

on wild mushroom cake with truffle sauce

for the truffle sauce
400ml game stock
5g dried ceps
2 level tbsp double cream
20g unsalted butter
1 dash of truffle essence
salt and pepper
720g venison saddle, boned and trimmed

for the wild mushroom cake
20g unsalted butter
250g wild mushrooms, thinly sliced
150ml milk
1 clove of garlic, crushed
1 level dessertspoon cornflour
1 egg yolk
salt and pepper
nutmeg

For the truffle sauce: put game stock with dried ceps in saucepan over heat, bring to the boil, then simmer for about 30 minutes until reduced by half.

Add cream, then whisk in cold butter pieces until all is amalgamated.

Add truffle essence, then pass sauce through a fine sieve into another saucepan. Check seasoning, reserve until required.

Cut venison into portion slices (across saddle), each approximately 60g, to yield 3 medallions per person.

Put film of oil in sauté pan over heat. When hot, place medallions in pan and cook on one side for 1 minute to seal and get some texture on meat. Then turn over and cook for further 30 seconds to seal.

Place medallions on roasting tray and cook in preheated oven (220°C/gas mark 7) for 3–4 minutes. Medallions should be pink in centre.

For the wild mushroom cake: melt butter in sauté pan. Add mushrooms, stir gently until mushrooms begin to sweat, then add milk, stirring again. Add garlic, stir through mushrooms. Sprinkle cornflour over mushrooms, stirring in until all absorbed by milk.

Remove from heat, beat egg yolk, then add to mushrooms, stirring into mixture. Season to taste and add a little nutmeg. Reserve until required in warm oven.

To serve, spoon 3 small amounts of mushroom cake on to warm serving plate. Place 1 medallion of venison on top of each cake, then spoon truffle sauce over each medallion. Serve with mixed, seasonal vegetables and potato.

David Wilson
The Peat Inn

Caramelised banana

on banana bread with coconut ice cream, coconut biscuit and caramel sauce

for the banana bread

2 ripe bananas
50g granulated sugar
100g melted butter
3 eggs
10g plain flour
1 level tsp baking powder

for the coconut biscuit

1¹/₂ egg whites
50g castor sugar
30g sifted plain flour
30g desiccated coconut
30g melted butter

for the coconut ice cream

150ml milk
150ml double cream
¹/₂ tsp liquid glucose
2 egg yolks
100g castor sugar
100ml coconut cream

for the caramel

100g castor sugar
100ml water
50ml boiling water

For the banana bread: peel bananas, roughly chop, place in food processor and work to a smooth purée. Pour mixture into bowl, add sugar and mix together. Add melted butter. Crack eggs into another bowl, lightly beat, then add to banana mixture. Add half flour and baking powder, mix together for about 1 minute then add remainder of flour, mixing until fully incorporated.

Place baking rings (80mm diameter) on non-stick baking sheet. Spoon mix into rings, approximately 10mm deep. Bake in preheated oven (175°C/gas mark 4) for about 20 minutes until risen slightly and golden brown. Turn on to a wire rack to cool.

For the coconut biscuit: whisk egg whites and sugar together as a meringue mix. Fold in sifted flour and coconut. Add melted butter. Spoon mix on to Silpat mat on baking sheet, spread to round shape approximately 80mm in diameter (to make 4 biscuits). Bake in preheated oven (210°C/gas mark 7) until light golden colour, remove using a spatula and place on wire rack to cool. If not using immediately store in airtight container.

For the coconut ice cream: bring milk and cream to the boil and add liquid glucose. Whisk egg yolks and sugar together until pale in colour. Slowly add boiled milk/cream mix to egg mix, whisk together. Place pan in double boiler (if you don't have one, put the pan in a bigger pan with water inside it) over heat, stirring constantly until mixture coats back of spoon. Remove pan from double boiler, place in large bowl with cold water and ice. Once cooled, add coconut cream.

For the caramel sauce: place sugar and water in heavy-bottomed pan. Bring to the boil and make caramel, which should be golden tan in colour. Add boiling water, stir together. Set aside until required.

David Wilson
The Peat Inn

for the coconut/caramel sauce

100g castor sugar
100ml water
150ml double cream
100ml coconut cream

for the banana tuille

1 egg white
1 medium banana
4 bananas

For the coconut/caramel sauce: put sugar and water in pan, bring to the boil to caramelise. The colour should be golden tan. Add cream and coconut cream, stirring together over heat for about 2 minutes. Reserve until required.

For the banana tuille: purée banana and egg white together until smooth. Spread on to Silpat mat on an oven sheet in a very thin layer. Bake in a preheated oven at 225°C/gas mark 7 for about 45 minutes or until set enough to cut. Cut into strips about 25mm x 100mm long. Lift strips from sheet to loosen then return to oven. Continue baking for a further 10–15 minutes until strong enough to shape. Twist to desired shape. Store in airtight container until required.

Peel bananas, slice into 9 pieces about $1/2$ inch thick. Pour some caramel into a large sauté pan over heat. Place banana pieces in caramel, cook for 2–3 minutes until one side of bananas is caramelised. Turn over and caramelise other side. Keep warm.

To serve, warm banana bread then place on centre of serving plate. Place approximately 6 slices of caramelised banana on top of bread, then coconut biscuit on top of banana segments.

Place 3 banana pieces at top and bottom of plate. Place ball of coconut ice cream on top of biscuit then decorate with banana tuille. Run coconut/caramel sauce around plate.

Serve immediately.

SCOTLAND ON A **PLATE**

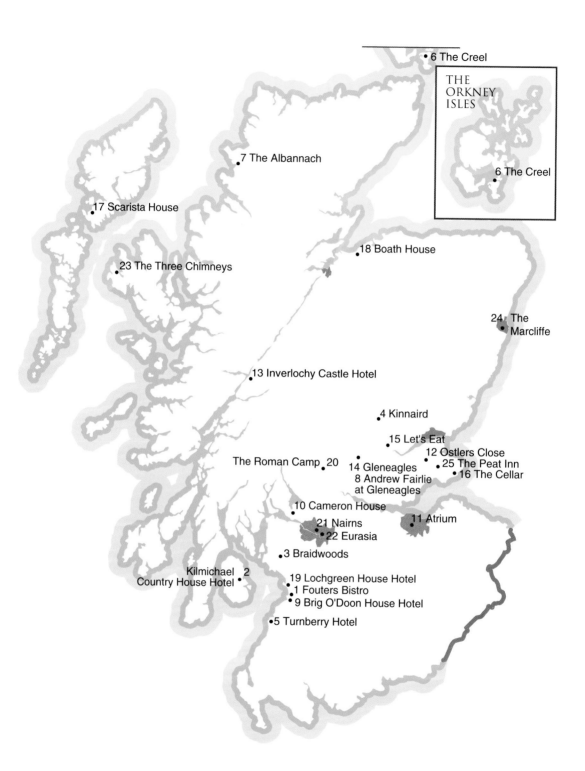

6 The Creel

THE
ORKNEY
ISLES

6 The Creel

7 The Albannach

17 Scarista House

23 The Three Chimneys

18 Boath House

24 The Marcliffe

13 Inverlochy Castle Hotel

4 Kinnaird

15 Let's Eat

12 Ostlers Close

The Roman Camp 20

14 Gleneagles
8 Andrew Fairlie
at Gleneagles

25 The Peat Inn
16 The Cellar

10 Cameron House

21 Nairns

11 Atrium

22 Eurasia

3 Braidwoods

Kilmichael
Country House Hotel 2

19 Lochgreen House Hotel
1 Fouters Bistro
9 Brig O'Doon House Hotel

5 Turnberry Hotel

Contributors

1 **Fouters Bistro**
2A Academy Street
Ayr
Tel. 01292 261391

2 **Kilmichael Country House Hotel**
Glencloy
Brodick
Isle of Arran
Tel. 01770 302219

3 **Braidwoods**
Drumastle Mill Cottage
Dalry
Ayrshire
Tel. 01294 833544

4 **Kinnaird**
Kinnaird Estate
By Dunkeld
Perthshire
Tel. 01796 482440

5 **Turnberry Hotel**
Turnberry
Ayrshire
Tel. 01655 331000

6 **The Creel**
Front Road
St Margaret's Hope
Orkney
Tel. 01856 831311

7 **The Albannach**
Baddidarroch
Lochinver
Sutherland
Tel. 01571 844407

8 **Andrew Fairlie at Gleneagles**
Gleaneagles Hotel
Auchterarder
Perthshire
Tel. 01764 694267

9 **Brig O'Doon House Hotel**
Alloway
Ayr
Tel. 01292 442466

10 **Cameron House**
Loch Lomond
Dunbartonshire
Tel. 01389 755565

11 **Atrium**
10 Cambridge Street
Edinburgh
Tel. 0131 228 8882

12 **Ostlers Close**
25 Bonnygate
Cupar
Fife
Tel. 01334 655574

13 **Inverlochy Castle Hotel**
Torlundy
Fort William
Inverness-shire
Tel. 01397 702177

14 **Gleneagles Hotel**
Auchterarder
Perthshire
Tel. 01764 662231

15 **Let's Eat**
77 Kinnoull Street
Perth
Tel. 01738 643377

16 **The Cellar**
24 East Green
Anstruther
Fife
Tel. 01333 310378

17 **Scarista House**
Isle of Harris
Western Isles
Tel. 01859 550238

18 **Boath House**
Auldearn
By Nairn
Highland
Tel. 01667 454896

19 **Lochgreen House Hotel**
Monktonhill Road
Southwood
Troon
Ayrshire
Tel. 01292 313343

20 **The Roman Camp Hotel**
off Main Street
Callander
Perthshire
Tel. 01877 330003

21 **Nairns**
13 Woodside Crescent
Glasgow
G3 7UL
Tel. 0141 353 0707

22 **Eurasia**
150 St Vincent Street
Glasgow
G2 5NE
Tel. 0141 204 1150

23 **The Three Chimneys**
Colbost
Dunvegan
Isle of Skye
Tel. 01470 511258

24 **The Marcliffe at Pitfodels**
North Deeside Road
Aberdeen
Tel. 01224 861000

25 **The Peat Inn**
Peat Inn
Fife
Tel. 01334 840206

Index

Asparagus, puff pastry, pillow of — 126

Asparagus mousse — 34

Banana, caramelised — 258

Beef, Aberdeen Angus, carpaccio — 220

Beef, Angus, fillet of — 38

Beef, Buccleuch, medallion of — 48

Beef, fillet, with onion marmalade — 54

Beef, fillet, with roasted garlic butter — 247

Beef and mushrooms with herb crust — 130

Biscuit, hot chocolate, with vanilla ice cream — 82

Chicken, farmhouse, baked breast of — 99

Chicken, tournedos, stuffed — 19

Chicken livers, parfait of — 4

Cod, coriander-crusted — 151

Cod, roast supreme of — 223

Crab, Anstruther, dressed — 252

Crab, green, bisque — 56

Crab, hot spiced Arran — 15

Crab tian, Three Chimneys Skye — 230

Duck, leg, crisp roast confit — 28

Game, wild, ballotine of — 90

Grouse, roast breast of — 81

Grouse, young — 182

Guinea fowl, corn-fed, supremes — 172

Haggis millefeuille — 47

Halibut, fillet — 255

Halibut, grilled — 161

Kidneys with two mustards — 16

Lamb best end — 205

Lamb, Carrick, with fine ratatouille — 8

Lamb, hill-fed Highland, roast fillet — 64

Lamb, grilled loin of — 232

Lamb, Perthshire, loin of — 110

Langoustines and crowdie malfatti — 168

Lemon curd, baked — 144

Lobster, roasted — 200

Lobster, Scottish — 136

Lobster, Sound of Harris — 171

Lobster, vanille, grilled — 236

Millefeuilles, honey wafer of, raspberries and nectarines — 31

Monkfish, seared — 214

Mousse, bitter chocolate — 50

Mousse, white chocolate — 206

Mussels, with a shallot, thyme and garlic broth — 158

Omelette, cep — 188

Parfait, iced damson — 239

Parfait, praline — 163

Partridge, pan-fried — 213

Partridge, Perthshire, roast — 152

Peaches, roast 133

Pig's trotter, stuffed 121

Pomme, ratte 106

Potato, baked, with cod 86

Ravioli, of scallop with red pesto 96

Rice pudding, caramelised 113

Roulade, chocolate 175

Salmon, confit of 178

Salmon, escalope, hot smoked 24

Salmon, Marrbury, smoked 78

Scallops, baked, in their shells 77

Scallops, Isle of Mull, seared 116

Scallops, Loch Broom, hand-dived 66

Scallops, pan-seared 242

Scallops, Skye, gratin 148

Scallops, West Coast 7

Sea bass, with artichoke ravioli 37

Sea bass, wild, seared 141

Seafood broth 44

Seafood, lightly curried selection 89

Shellfish and saffron broth 210

Shortcake, strawberry 61

Smokie, Arbroath, and saffron stew 27

Soufflé, chocolate 227

Soufflé, chocolate, hot 248

Soufflé, iced, with Grand Marnier 9

Soufflé, iced praline and Amaretto 155

Soufflé, roast red pepper 70

Soufflé, vanilla 40

Soufflés, raspberry, hot 217

Soup, lightly curried 224

Soup, pea 181

Sponge, steamed tayberry and syrup 123

Squab poached in cep broth 203

Sundae, gin and damson 20

Sweets, Lochgreen, assiette of 196

Tart, dark chocolate 103

Tart, sweetbread, with noisettes of
Ayrshire lamb 194

Tart, thin, of seared strawberries 93

Terrine, pan-fried, of potato and duck leg 118

Torte, chocolate truffle 184

Torte, lime, with berry baskets 72

Tuna, seared 162

Turbot, fillet of 100

Turbot, Mallaig, with roasted Scottish
lobster 129

Turbot, roasted, fillet of 109

Veal, medallions of 190

Veal, roasted fillet 140

Venison, saddle, medallions of 256

Venison, striploin, roasted 245

Wolf-fish, roasted, and skate wings 58

Weights, measures and servings

All weights, measures and servings are approximate conversions

Solid weight conversions

Metric	Imperial
10g	½ oz
20g	¾ oz
25g	1 oz
40g	1½ oz
50g	2 oz
60g	2½ oz
75g	3 oz
110g	4 oz
125g	4½ oz
150g	5 oz
175g	6 oz
200g	7 oz
225g	8 oz
250g	9 oz
275g	10 oz
350g	12 oz
450g	1 lb
700g	1½ lb
900g	2 lb
1.35kg	3 lb

Liquid conversions

Metric	Imperial
55ml	2 fl.oz
75ml	3 fl.oz
150ml	5 fl.oz (¼ pint)
275ml	½ pint
425ml	¾ pint
570ml	1 pint
725ml	1¼ pints
1 litre	1¾ pints
1.2 litre	2 pints
1.5 litre	2½ pints
2.25 litre	4 pints

Standards liquid

1 tsp	=	5ml
1 tbsp	=	15ml
1 fl.oz	=	30ml
1 pint	=	20 fl.oz
1 litre	=	35 fl.oz

Standards solid

1 oz	=	25g
1 lb	=	16 oz
1 g	=	0.35 oz
1 kg	=	2.2 lb

Oven temperature conversions

°C	Gas	°F
140	1	275
150	2	300
170	3	325
180	4	350
190	5	375
200	6	400
220	7	425
230	8	450
240	9	475